D0646518

the el paso chile company's texas border cookbook

home cooking

from rio grande

country

w. park kerr

and norma kerr

and michael

mclaughlin

william morrow and company, inc.
new york

Sweet Texas Fire, Snakebite Salsa,
and Texas Trash are trademarks of
the El Paso Chile Company.

Copyright © 1992 by W. Park Kerr and Norma Kerr and Michael McLaughlin

All rights reserved. No part of this book may be reproduced or utilized in any form or by any means, electronic or mechanical, including photocopying, recording, or by any information storage or retrieval system, without permission in writing from the Publisher. Inquiries should be addressed to Permissions Department, William Morrow and Company, Inc., 1350 Avenue of the Americas, New York, N.Y. 10019.

It is the policy of William Morrow and Company, Inc., and its imprints and affiliates, recognizing the importance of preserving what has been written, to print the books we publish on acid-free paper, and we exert our best efforts to that end.

Library of Congress Cataloging-in-Publication Data

Kerr, W. Park.
    The El Paso Chile Company's Texas border cookbook : home cooking
  from Rio Grande country / by W. Park and Norma Kerr and Michael McLaughlin.
        p.   cm.
    Includes bibliographical references and index.
    ISBN 0-688-10941-1
    1. Cookery—Texas—El Paso Region.   2. Cookery, American—
  Southwestern style.   I. El Paso Chile Company.   II. Kerr, Norma.
  III. El Paso Chile Company.   IV. Title.
  TX715.K3783   1992
  641.59764'96—dc20
                                                              92-265
                                                              CIP

Printed in the United States of America

First Edition

02 03 04 05 06 QW 20 19 18 17 16 15 14 13 12 11

BOOK DESIGN CONCEPT BY LESLIE PIRTLE

to Martina Marie Lorey
for not divorcing Park during
the writing of this book

and to
William Park Kerr, Sr., husband and father, with love

acknowledgments

Our business and this book are the result of a dream we had twelve years ago, a dream of bringing the food of El Paso to the widest possible audience. Between the dream and the reality many people—more than we can adequately acknowledge—shared advice, cash, and friendship. Among them we would most especially like to thank:

Our friends who became our first customers, and our customers who became our friends and supported us over the years.

Our loyal staff, all of whom bring new meaning to the expression "family business."

The retailers, large and small, who stock our products in their stores and whose passion for the hot stuff keeps us going.

Lora Belle Godwin, Consuelo and Gina Forti, The Rubio family, and Kay Quevedo, for feeding us so well and so often, for sharing their knowledge of El Paso's food, and for loaning us a recipe or two.

The enthusiastic crowd of hungry relatives, friends, and neighbors who came to eat and critique all during a long hot summer of recipe testing.

Mary Margaret Davis, Barbara Sykes Aksamit, Harl Dixon, Mary Frances Allen, the *El Paso Times,* the *Herald Post,* John Werner, Michelle Lorey, family and friends at Lomart Grocery Store, Amy Campbell Lamphere, and Francine Maroukian, all of whom had, variously, something significant to do with getting this book into your hands.

Johnnie Rogers, Jr., who loaned us much more than mere money.

Leslie and Woody Pirtle, and Lisa Haney, for their crayons, pencils, endless good humor, and the armadillo.

Our publicists, Lisa Ekus and David Nussbaum, for generating endless excitement and piles and piles of clippings.

Our editor, Maria Guarnaschelli, who knew Tex-Mex wasn't dead, and rolled up her sleeves to help us prove it.

Everyone at William Morrow for designing our works into a beautiful book and Skip Dye, for selling the hell out of it.

contents

contents

el paso: geography as destiny

El Paso was originally El Paso del Norte—the pass of the north—and here on the Rio Grande, at one of the few (some say the only) year-round snow-free passes across the Rocky Mountains, lies a city that is defined by its geography. ✦ Founded by Juan de Oñate as he traveled north along the Camino Real—the old king's highway—on his way to establishing the city of Santa Fe, El Paso has always had more than one personality. ✦ At the corner (as the tourist ads say) of Texas and Old Mexico, modern El Paso is unique. ✦ Isolated, located far to the "left" of what for many years was the largest state, El Paso partakes of the lore and legend of Texas without really giving in to it all the way. ✦ Other strong influences lie closer at hand, and here on the U.S. border, facing Juárez, a major Mexican city of over a million people, and with the state of New Mexico only a few miles to our north, El Paso blends Texas, New Mexico, and Old Mexico into a cultural cocktail that seems very much the best of all possible worlds. ✦ Texans think we're New Mexican. ✦ New Mexico thinks we're confused. ✦ And we're just glad to be here, thanks, where the food and the weather and the people are wonderful.

It is here, that we, as eighth- and ninth-generation Texans, members of a family that settled in the West before Texas was even a state (yes, ancestors died at the Alamo), chose to found The El Paso Chile Company. Twelve years ago, Park had just left college, and Norma, who had raised two children, was a wife and a part-time water-colorist, as well as a renowned local cook. Putting the desire for our own business together with our passion for food—especially for the local blend of west Texas and Mexican food—we started out selling *ristras*, those decorative and useful strings of dried red chiles, on street corners. Our first packaged product was a chili powder seasoning blend, designed to help cooks re-create Norma's famous quick and easy chili. Salsas, barbecue sauces, snacks, and condiments soon followed as the line grew to become one of the major specialty food offerings in the country. From our very first food show, when we sold everything we brought, customers from little food shops to major department store chains to national catalogs have understood and appreciated what we were trying to do. Now, with this book, we have been given the opportunity to extend our passion for the food of El Paso into an entirely new area.

El Paso has a long tradition of home entertaining, one that blends the local food with other, more modern, less Texan influences. As busy working people living in a city not known, aside from a small handful of successes, as a restaurant town, we have always had to balance the demands of our careers with our desire to entertain well at home. And between us, with the differing viewpoints of two generations, we have evolved the recipes and menus that fill this book.

In one way or another, whether they reflect Texas, Mexico, or the developing cuisine known as New Southwestern, these recipes are based in authenticity, adapted by personal tastes, and have been chosen to let you entertain well, in the El Paso style, and to give you a real sense of what the local food is all about. Opening a jar of one of our products is like taking a first bite; opening the pages of this book and heading for the kitchen we hope will make you really want to tuck in. By the time you sit down to enjoy this food from the corner of Texas and Old Mexico, we trust you'll have come to appreciate, love, and even crave it as much as we do.

El Paso, Texas

chapter one

in the beginning
salsas, dips, appetizers, and snacks

In Texas, every place is a long way from every place else, and company always shows up hungry. This is not a recent development. Historically speaking, back when things were wild and woolly, it was important to distinguish between the arrival of tired, dusty, and famished strangers, who were merely greeted with the business end of a shotgun, and tired, dusty, and famished friends, who expected—and got—something good to eat pretty damned quick. Modern interstate highways and air-conditioned Mercedes-Benzes notwithstanding, the speedy production of some kind of zesty nibble or other is still the mark of a successful Texas host. When the sun sinks over the Rio Grande and the clink of ice and the whir of another blenderful of margaritas fill the air, the following little mouthfuls spell *bienvenidos,* El Paso style.

a passel of salsas

Fiery (and also complimentary) bowls of salsa are as common on Southwestern restaurant tables as salt and pepper shakers are elsewhere. Red or green, thick or thin, complex or simple, milder or red-hot, salsa is scooped up by crisp tostaditas or lavishly spooned over almost anything edible by Texas diners who look positively panicky when the bowl runs dry. An inexpensive giveaway but an essential condiment, every salsa is slightly different, expressing each chef's regional preferences and individuality. Home cooks in El Paso also whip up salsas, each as distinctive as its whipper-upper. A few fresh, simple ingredients and the assistance of a blender or a sharp knife are all it takes, and even though we're in the bottled salsa business, we think every cook should know how to produce so essential a kitchen staple from scratch. Here is a passel of our favorite salsas, the very ones that inspired our business in the first place.

pico de gallo
(chunky raw salsa)

Very *picante* and thick with crunchy vegetables, this is El Paso's (and the Kerr clan's) favorite fresh salsa. One version, served with the fajitas at the Tigua Indian Cultural Center Restaurant, is little more than raw chunks of jalapeño, tomato, and onion—a crisp, delicious salad/relish. Our pico de gallo is somewhat more liquid than that but otherwise retains its essential crunchy texture and high-thermostat setting. If you have let your big kitchen knife get dull, now is the time to sharpen it up—this is just not the same salsa when the ingredients are chopped by machine.

The name, by the way, translates as "rooster's beak," possibly a reference to the decidedly sharp nature of the salsa, and is shared with a central Mexican salad of chili-powder-dusted jicama and oranges. Many El Paso cooks use local yellow peppers (page 248) but jalapeños work just fine.

6 long green chiles
2 large ripe tomatoes (about 1
    pound), cored, seeded, and
    coarsely hand-chopped
1 cup coarsely chopped onion
⅓ cup minced cilantro

2 to 3 fresh yellow chiles or large
    fresh jalapeño chiles, stemmed
    and coarsely hand-chopped
3 tablespoons fresh lime juice
¾ teaspoon salt

In the open flame of a gas burner or under a preheated broiler, roast the long green chiles, turning them, until they are lightly but evenly charred. Steam the chiles in a paper bag, or in a bowl, covered with a plate, until cool. Rub away the burned peel. Stem and seed the chiles and coarsely chop them. There should be about 1 cup.

In a medium bowl, stir together the tomatoes, chopped green chiles, onions, cilantro, yellow chiles, lime juice, and salt. Cover and refrigerate 1 hour. Adjust the seasoning. *Though the salsa will lose some of its texture, the flavor will remain good for up to 2 days.*

makes 2½ cups

salsa del norte
(roasted tomato salsa with green chiles)

A short ingredient list means that even slight changes in technique make a huge difference in the finished dish. In this nubbly, red salsa, broiling the tomatoes adds a subtle but wonderful smoky quality that makes for addictive eating. The chopped green chiles aren't essential, but they are a fine addition to a typical Chihuahua-style salsa.

4 long green chiles	3 to 5 chiles de arbol, stemmed and
2 large ripe tomatoes (about 1	crumbled
pound)	2 garlic cloves, peeled and chopped
¼ cup water	½ teaspoon salt
2 tablespoons fresh lime juice	¼ cup minced cilantro

In the open flame of a gas burner or under a preheated broiler, roast the long green chiles, turning them, until they are lightly but evenly charred. Steam the chiles in a paper bag, or in a bowl, covered with a plate, until cool. Rub away the burned peel. Stem and seed the chiles and coarsely chop them. There should be about ⅔ cup.

Adjust the rack to about 6 inches from the heat source and preheat the broiler. On a shallow pan (like a cookie sheet), broil the tomatoes, turning them once or twice, until the peels are evenly charred, about 20 minutes. Cool them to room temperature. Remove and discard the cores; chop the tomato flesh and peel.

In a blender, combine the water, lime juice, chiles de arbol, garlic, and salt, and blend on high speed until smooth. Add the tomatoes, with all the juice and charred peels, and blend on low speed until smooth. Transfer to a bowl, stir in the green chiles and cilantro, and refrigerate, covered, for at least 1 hour. Adjust the seasoning. *The salsa can be prepared up to 2 days ahead without loss of texture or flavor.*

For *Chipotle Salsa del Norte,* replace the chiles de arbol with 3 or 4 chipotles adobado, including the clinging sauce. Proceed as directed.

makes 2½ cups

a grill supper

Pitchers of White Sangria (page 241)

Queso Fundido on the Grill (page 20) with Soft Corn Tortillas
Grilled Shrimp with Smoked Jalapeño Mayonnaise (pages 22 and 23)

Beef Tacos al Carbón (page 42) with
Mantequilla de los Pobres (page 11)
and Salsa del Norte (page 4)
Ensalada de Nopalitos (page 202)
Texas Three-Bean Salad (page 200)

Norma's Quick and Easy Frozen Mango Dessert (page 232)
Bizcochos (page 220)

santos's salsa verde
(tomatillo and green chile salsa)

Green salsas are perhaps slightly less common than red, but no less welcome, and chile heads eat them with equal relish. (In the best of all possible restaurants, in the best of all possible worlds, *both* types of salsa are on the table at once, and neither *ever* runs out.) If you have not eaten a green salsa before, the brilliant color and distinctive acidic and herbal taste will be a revelation. This recipe is from Santos Roman, who has "done" for both Kerr households for years.

3 long green chiles	1 garlic clove, peeled and chopped
1 pound (about 12) fresh tomatillos, husked	¾ teaspoon salt
½ cup water	½ cup finely chopped white onion
	¼ cup minced cilantro

In the open flame of a gas burner or under a preheated broiler, roast the long green chiles, turning them, until they are lightly but evenly charred. Steam the chiles in a paper bag, or in a bowl, covered with a plate, until cool. Rub away the burned peel. Stem and seed the chiles and coarsely chop them. There should be about ½ cup.

In a medium saucepan, cover the tomatillos with water. Set the pan over medium heat, bring to a simmer, and cook, uncovered, about 10 minutes, or until the tomatillos are soft. Drain and cool them.

In a blender, combine the tomatillos, green chiles, water, garlic, and salt, and purée on high speed until smooth. Transfer to a bowl and stir in the onions and cilantro. Cover and refrigerate for at least 1 hour. Adjust the seasoning. *The salsa can be prepared up to 2 days ahead without loss of flavor or texture.*

makes 2½ cups

corn, black bean, and
roasted red pepper salsa

Bean salsas are part of the Southwestern new wave. Some of this experimental cuisine is just silly (send us a stamped, self-addressed envelope for a list of the dopiest dishes we've found), but we love bean salsas, and judging by the dozens of bottled versions available, so does the American public. Here is a recipe better than anything you'll find for sale. Though it's reasonably uncomplicated, you may speed things up even further by substituting 2½ cups of well-drained canned beans for the cooked dried beans. (The flavor and texture are not quite the same but the convenience is undeniable.) This is only as hot as the salsa you use. For extra fire add two finely chopped pickled jalapeños. Serve this chunky, brilliantly colored mélange with tostaditas and drinks or use it as a relish/garnish with grilled fish, chicken, beef, or pork.

1 cup dried black beans, picked
    over and rinsed
2 teaspoons salt
1 large heavy sweet red pepper
1½ cups thick tomato-based bottled
    hot salsa

1½ cups corn kernels, canned or
    defrosted frozen, well drained
3 green onions, trimmed and sliced
    (about ½ cup)
About 1 cup canned tomato juice
½ cup minced cilantro

In a medium bowl, combine the beans with water to cover by at least 3 inches and let them soak overnight.

Drain the beans. In a medium saucepan, combine the beans with water to cover by at least 3 inches. Set over medium heat, bring to a simmer, and cook, uncovered, stirring once or twice, for 30 minutes. Stir in the salt and cook another 20 to 30 minutes, or until just tender. Drain and cool them.

In the open flame of a gas burner or under a preheated broiler, roast the pepper, turning it often, until the peel is charred. In a closed paper bag, or in a bowl covered with a plate, steam the pepper until cool. Rub away the charred peel, stem and core the pepper, and cut the flesh into ¼-inch dice.

In a medium bowl, combine the beans, roasted red pepper, bottled salsa, corn, and green onions.

Add enough tomato juice to give the mixture a loose, salsalike texture (the amount will depend on the thickness of the bottled salsa you have chosen). Stir in the cilantro. Cover and refrigerate at least 1 hour. Adjust the seasoning. *The salsa can be prepared up to 2 days ahead.*

makes 6 cups

tropical mango salsa

This is another new wave salsa, a direct descendant of many Mexican dishes that combine fruit and chiles with sweetly fiery results. It's not intended to be eaten with tostaditas, but does make the perfect garnish for grilled fish (especially salmon and tuna), chicken, or pork. Mangoes, once available for the most part only seasonally, are increasingly available much of the year, but papaya or fresh pineapple can be substituted and, in summer, so can peaches or nectarines.

1 medium-size ripe mango (about ¾ pound)
1¼ cups tomato-based bottled hot salsa

2 green onions, trimmed and sliced (about ⅓ cup)
¼ cup minced cilantro

Peel the mango. Cut the flesh away from the pit and coarsely dice it.

In a medium bowl, stir together the diced mango, bottled salsa, green onions, and cilantro. Cover and refrigerate at least 1 hour. Adjust the seasoning. *The salsa can be prepared up to 1 day ahead without loss of texture or flavor.*

makes 2½ cups

dips and dunks

Beyond salsas, the Texas table holds other dippy starters, some serving as clear-cut appetizers, others with various roles. (*Versatile guacamole, for example, turns up as a sauce, a stuffing, or a salad about as often as it does as a dip.*) *All are intensely colorful and zesty palate-awakeners, most are accompanied by tostaditas or corn tortillas, and, if a measure of self-control is maintained, all set the diner up for the delicious main course to follow.* Here are our favorites.

guacamole

Guacamole, the salad/sauce of avocado, tomato, chiles, onion, and cilantro, is at its best when at its simplest—which doesn't mean there isn't room for a secret ingredient. As with other successful clandestine culinary tricks, a generous dollop of Miracle Whip doesn't at all harm the guacamole, and even contributes a welcome touch of acidity. It may also slow the inevitable discoloring of the gorgeous green stuff. Use Hass avocados—the smaller, bumpy black-skinned kind. Those large, watery, stringy, and generally tasteless bright green avocados grown in Florida are not even offered for sale in El Paso.

1 cup roughly chopped cilantro (some stems may be included)

2 fresh jalapeño chiles, stemmed and chopped

1 teaspoon salt

4 large buttery-ripe black-skinned avocados (about 2 pounds), pitted and peeled

1 pound (5 or 6) ripe plum tomatoes, halved, seeded, and diced

½ cup diced red onion

¼ cup Kraft Miracle Whip Salad Dressing

In a blender or a small food processor, purée together the cilantro, jalapeños, and salt until smooth.

In a medium bowl, roughly mash the avocados. Stir in the cilantro purée, tomatoes, onions, and Miracle Whip. Adjust the seasoning.

Cover with plastic wrap, pressing the film onto the surface of the guacamole. *Store it at room temperature for up to 30 minutes, or refrigerate it for up to 3 hours.*

makes 3 cups

mantequilla de los pobres
(butter of the poor—mashed avocado purée)

"Poor" hardly describes with accuracy the lucky folks who get to substitute delicious mashed avocado for ordinary butter. Reverse food humor aside, the purée is frequently used as a garnish or accompaniment, where the more complicated flavors of guacamole are not appropriate. We prefer it with fajitas and sometimes offer a bowl of Mantequilla de los Pobres, a bowl of Pico de Gallo (page 3), and a basket of warm, fresh Tostaditas (page 32) as a rustically informal, mix-and-match appetizer.

4 buttery-ripe black-skinned avocados, pitted and peeled

¾ teaspoon salt
½ teaspoon freshly ground black pepper

In a medium bowl, coarsely mash the avocados. Stir in the salt and freshly ground pepper. Adjust the seasoning. This "butter" is best served immediately but can be held at room temperature, covered by a piece of plastic wrap pressed onto its surface, for 1 hour.

makes about 2 cups

chile con queso
(hot cheese and chile dip)

Chile con queso comes in several forms—all delicious. At its most elemental, it is queso fundido ("melted cheese") (page 20). At its most blatantly Tex-Mex, it is a deliciously gooey, Day-Glo-orange processed cheese concoction (in fact, we manufacture an excellent rendition). Somewhere else on the spectrum is the following version. This Chihuahua-style chile con queso, based on the one we regularly devour at a favorite restaurant, Rubio's, is a rich and brothy affair, loaded with pully Monterey Jack cheese and eaten spooned onto soft, warm corn tortillas or scooped up with tostaditas. The liquid base can be prepared several days ahead; the final reheating and the melting of the cheese take only minutes. Should there be any "CCQ" left (an unlikely occurrence in our experience), it can be reheated in a microwave oven and used as a sublime sauce over scrambled eggs.

6 long green chiles	1½ cups chicken broth, homemade or canned
3 tablespoons olive oil	½ cup canned crushed tomatoes with added purée
1 cup chopped onion	¾ pound Monterey Jack cheese, cubed
2 to 4 fresh jalapeño chiles, stemmed and sliced into rounds	Corn tortillas or Tostaditas (page 32), warmed
3 garlic cloves, peeled and minced	
½ teaspoon oregano, crumbled	

In the open flame of a gas burner or under a preheated broiler, roast the long green chiles, turning them, until they are lightly but evenly charred. Steam the chiles in a paper bag, or in a bowl, covered with a plate, until cool. Rub away the burned peel. Stem and seed the chiles and coarsely chop them. There should be about 1 cup.

In a medium saucepan over low heat, warm the olive oil. Add the onions, jalapeños, garlic, and oregano and cook, covered, until the onions are translucent, about 7 minutes. Add the chicken broth, tomatoes, and chopped green chiles and bring to a simmer. Partially cover and cook, stirring once or twice, for 15 minutes. *The recipe can be prepared to this point 3 days ahead. Cool it and refrigerate, covered.*

Over low heat, bring the broth mixture to a simmer. Stir in the cheese, cover the pan, and cook, stirring once or twice, until the cheese is just melted and is "stringing." Transfer the chile con queso to a bowl and serve immediately, accompanied by corn tortillas or tostaditas.

serves 4 to 6

kay queveda's
chile con queso with crab

Even people who love to cook sometimes need the services of a caterer, and when we find ourselves in that position we usually call Kay Queveda, one of El Paso's best. Among Kay's specialities is this chile con queso, combining pickled jalapeños, artichoke hearts, and sweet crabmeat in a luscious base of melted cream cheese and sour cream. It is a completely different way of thinking about and cooking chile con queso, and it is so easy and so deliciously habit forming we convinced her to share the recipe. Kay serves it hot in a chafing dish and accompanies it with toasted pita bread triangles, but tostaditas (sturdy ones—it's a thick, chunky dip) work well too.

1 pound cream cheese, cubed
½ cup liquid from a jar of pickled
    jalapeño chiles
4 to 6 pickled jalapeño chiles,
    stemmed and sliced into thin
    rounds
2 14-ounce cans artichoke hearts in
    water, drained and quartered
8 ounces sour cream

1 pound fresh jumbo-lump crab-
    meat, picked over, or 3 6-ounce
    cans crabmeat, drained
½ cup grated Parmesan cheese
Salt to taste
Freshly ground white pepper to
    taste
Toasted pita bread triangles or
    Tostaditas (page 32)

In a medium heavy pan over low heat, combine the cream cheese, jalapeño liquid, and pickled jalapeños and cook, stirring occasionally, until the cheese has just melted. Stir in the artichoke hearts and sour cream and continue to cook, stirring often, until the mixture is hot. Stir in the crabmeat and Parmesan cheese, add salt and freshly ground white pepper to taste, and cook until the mixture just simmers (do not boil). Transfer to a chafing dish over a warming burner and serve.

serves 12

a new year's eve party

Domaine Cheurlin Brut New Mexico NV

Salsa del Norte (page 4) and Corn, Black Bean, and Roasted Red Pepper Salsa (page 7) and Guacamole (page 10) with Tostaditas (page 32) and Chicharrones

Kay Queveda's Chile con Queso with Crab (page 13) and Toasted Pita Triangles

Thin Chicken Flautas with Avocado Sauce (pages 45 and 46)

Deep-Fried Stuffed Jalapeños (page 24)

Ham and Hot Pepper Jelly Sandwiches on Mini Masa Biscuits (page 192)

Apple-Marinated Hickory-Smoked Turkey Breast (page 82) and Smoked Jalapeño-Lime Mayonnaise (page 23) Sandwiches on Small Hard Rolls

Mugs of Cream of Green Chile Soup (page 101)

Border Brownies (page 217)
Bizcochos (page 220)
Pineapple-Apricot Empanaditas (page 224)
Lemon-Lime Cookies (page 219)

rancho bean dip

This easy appetizer is a great illustration of our Pot Bean Rule: If you have a pot of beans, you'll find a use for them and if you don't, well, you won't. We often double this rich and creamy bean dip when there's a crowd on the way.

2 cups Frijoles de Olla (page 178), with liquid

½ cup canned crushed tomatoes with added purée

2 or 3 pickled jalapeño chiles or chiles chipotles *adobado,* stemmed and minced

½ cup grated Monterey Jack cheese or mozzarella cheese or a combination of both

½ cup grated medium-sharp cheddar cheese

2 green onions, trimmed and sliced (about ⅓ cup), for garnish

⅓ cup grated feta cheese, for garnish

12 corn tortillas or Tostaditas (page 32), warmed

In a small saucepan over medium heat, combine the beans and their liquid, the tomatoes, and jalapeños. Bring to a simmer and cook, uncovered, stirring and roughly mashing the beans occasionally, for about 15 minutes, or until the mixture is thick and creamy. Stir in the Monterey Jack and cheddar cheeses and heat, stirring, just until the cheeses are melted.

Transfer the dip to a wide, shallow dish that has been warmed, sprinkle it with the green onions and feta, and serve immediately, accompanied by corn tortillas or tostaditas.

serves 4 to 6

other good stuff

After salsas and dips, Texas cooks look to slightly fancier fare. *From crunchy munches like Texas Trash to fairly stylish grilled shrimp appetizers, the best of these snacks are zesty (we mean hot) and fairly quick to produce. Try any or all of the following at your next jamboree.*

texas trash

This is our Texas take on that universal back-of-the-package favorite, Chex Party Mix. The folks at Ralston Purina naturally feel that their version is the best (it's certainly the original), but in El Paso if it isn't hotted up some it isn't worth eating. We think we've stuffed every possible Texas ingredient into the following recipe, but if you come up with something we've left out, just throw it in—it's a very flexible and forgiving recipe. Though some people keep their Trash around in a big old tin for weeks, we prefer it freshly made, and anyway, there are almost never leftovers.

¾ stick (6 tablespoons) unsalted butter	2 cups Ritz Bits mini cheese crackers
¼ cup hot pepper sauce	2 cups Corn Nuts
2 tablespoons Worcestershire sauce	1½ cups fish-shaped pretzel crackers
1 tablespoon chili powder blend	
1 teaspoon oregano, crumbled	1 cup pepitas (roasted pumpkin seeds)
2 cups regular-size Fritos corn chips	1 cup roasted hulled peanuts
2 cups Crispix cereal	⅔ cup shelled sunflower seeds

Position a rack in the middle of the oven and preheat the oven to 250°F.

In a shallow 3-quart baking dish, melt together the butter, hot pepper sauce, Worcestershire sauce, chili powder blend, and oregano.

In a large bowl, stir together the Fritos, Crispix, Ritz Bits, Corn Nuts, pretzel crackers, *pepitas,* peanuts, and sunflower seeds. Add the Fritos mixture to the melted butter mixture in the baking dish and toss to coat it thoroughly and evenly.

Return the dish to the oven and bake, stirring every 10 minutes, for 1 hour. The Trash should be dry, loose, and lightly browned.

Transfer it to a storage container, cool it completely, and cover it tightly. Store at room temperature. The texture and flavor of the Texas Trash will be at their best when it is consumed within forty-eight hours.

makes 12 cups, serving many

quesadillas
(cheese and flour tortilla appetizers)

Quesadillas properly belong in the following chapter dedicated to tortilla cookery, but they are such an essential El Paso appetizer we have included them here instead. While deeper in Mexico *quesadilla* is correctly applied to a little filled turnover made of soft masa-based dough, in the U.S. border states (as in many Mexican and Tex-Mex restaurants around the country) quesadillas are some type of flour-tortilla-and-cheese combination. The El Paso quesadilla consists of two tortillas, sandwiching cheese and other savory elements, griddled, fried, or baked until melted and served cut into wedges. We like a bowl of Pico de Gallo (page 3) close at hand—the combination of crisp tortilla, warm, pully cheese, and fiery, crunchy salsa is wonderful. Quesadillas are a splendid catchall for such premium leftovers as grilled shrimp or chicken, and we're creative enough to serve them at meals ranging from brunch to a late-night snack. Bone-weary and ravenous after a hard day, we have even enjoyed a quesadilla and a green salad as a simple and comforting supper.

2 poblano chiles or 4 long green chiles	¾ pound Monterey Jack cheese, thinly sliced
Nonstick cooking spray	2 green onions, trimmed and sliced
4 10-inch flour tortillas	(about ⅓ cup)

In the open flame of a gas burner or under a preheated broiler, roast the poblanos, turning them, until they are lightly but evenly charred. Steam the chiles in a paper bag, or in a bowl, covered with a plate, until cool. Rub away the burned peel. Stem and seed the chiles and coarsely chop them. Cut the chiles into ¼-inch-wide strips.

Lightly spray a large nonstick skillet with nonstick spray and set over medium heat. Lay 1 tortilla in the skillet. Arrange half the cheese evenly over the tortilla, covering it completely. Scatter half the rajas and half the green onions evenly over the cheese. Top with a second tortilla. Spray the upper tortilla lightly with the nonstick spray. Weight the quesadilla with a plate and cook 2 to 3 minutes, or until the bottom tortilla is crisp and lightly browned. Remove the plate and, using a long spatula, turn the quesadilla. Weight it again and cook it another 2 to 3 minutes, or until the cheese is melted.

Slide the quesadilla onto a cutting board and cut it into 4 to 6 wedges. Transfer them to a plate and serve immediately. Repeat with the remaining ingredients.

Epazote Quesadillas In addition to or in place of the chile strips, sprinkle the cheese layer with about 1 teaspoon finely minced fresh epazote leaves (page 255). Cook as directed above.

Chorizo Quesadillas Use only 10 ounces of cheese. Scatter ¼ pound chorizo, cooked (page 252), over the cheese on each quesadilla along with or instead of the chile strips. Cook as directed above.

Grilled Shrimp or Chicken Quesadillas Use only 10 ounces of cheese. Scatter about ½ cup chopped Grilled Jalapeño Honey Mustard Chicken (page 86) or Grilled Shrimp (page 22) over the cheese on each quesadilla along with or instead of the chile strips. Cook as directed above.

serves 4 to 6

queso fundido on the grill
(melted cheese appetizer)

This dish elicits primitive reactions—eager, hungry people anxiously gathered around a small bowl, working feverishly to scoop the molten cheese onto warmed tortillas before it cools into a solid, still delicious but no longer flexible mass. Be certain your guests are seated and ready to go to work before rushing the queso fundido to the table. This is at its most authentic, we think, when made with border cheeses and baked on a charcoal grill, as it is in certain Juárez restaurants that specialize in cooking *al carbón*. You can approximate that effect by using American supermarket cheeses and a home grill, or you can prepare the dish under the broiler.

2 poblano chiles or 4 long green
    chiles
¾ pound melting cheese, preferably
    a combination of *asadero* and
    Chihuahua, in ½-inch dice

¼ pound chorizo, cooked (page 252)
12 corn tortillas or Tostaditas (page
    32), warmed

In the open flame of a gas burner or under a preheated broiler, roast the poblanos, turning them, until they are lightly but evenly charred. Steam the chiles in a paper bag, or in a bowl, covered with a plate, until cool. Rub away the burned peel. Stem and seed the chiles and cut them into ¼-inch-wide strips.

Light a charcoal fire and let it burn down until the coals are evenly white or preheat a gas grill (medium-high).

Combine the cheeses, chorizo, and chile strips in a disposable foil tin or metal grill-proof pan, set it on the grill rack, and cover the grill. Bake this about 5 minutes, or until the cheeses are melted but not browned and the chorizo is sizzling. Stir it once to combine it (the cheeses will be pully) and transfer it immediately to a small warmed bowl. Serve it at once, accompanied by corn tortillas or tostaditas.

For *Queso Fundido Americana,* use half low-moisture mozzarella and half Monterey Jack cheese in place of the Mexican cheeses. Use ¼ pound hot Italian-style sausage, crumbled and cooked, in place of the chorizo. Adjust the rack to about 6 inches from the heat source and preheat the broiler. Combine the cheeses, sausage, and chile strips in a shallow broiler-proof pan, set the pan under the broiler and cook about 5 minutes, or until the cheeses are melted but not browned and the sausage is sizzling. Stir it once to combine it, transfer it immediately to a small warmed bowl, and serve immediately.

serves 4 to 6

salsa shrimp cocktails

We serve these fiery, cilantro-spiked seafood cocktails in tall footed ice-cream parlor coupes (seviche is often served similarly in restaurants in Mexico), but you can use wineglasses or just arrange the shrimp mixture over the shredded romaine on small plates. As usual, the best-quality prepared salsa will produce the best results.

1½ pounds (about 36) medium
    shrimp, shelled and deveined
2 teaspoons salt
1 cup tomato-based bottled hot salsa
2 green onions, trimmed and sliced
    (about ¼ cup)

2 tablespoons minced cilantro
4 cups shredded romaine
2 buttery-ripe black-skinned
    avocados, pitted, peeled, and cut
    into eighths, for garnish

Bring a pot of water to a boil. Stir in the shrimp and salt and cook, stirring once or twice, until the shrimp are pink, curled, and just cooked through, about 4 minutes. Drain them immediately and cool them to room temperature.

In a medium bowl, combine the shrimp and salsa. Cover and let stand at room temperature for at least 30 minutes. *The recipe can be prepared to this point 1 day ahead then refrigerated. Return the shrimp mixture to room temperature before proceeding with the recipe.*

Stir the green onions and cilantro into the shrimp mixture and adjust the seasoning. Divide the shredded romaine among 8 footed coupe glasses. Spoon the shrimp mixture on top of the lettuce, dividing it evenly and using it all. Garnish each serving with 2 wedges of avocado and serve immediately.

serves 8

grilled shrimp

We use a gas grill which heats in minutes and admittedly makes turning out this delicious appetizer very quick. Charcoal-users will need to go through the lighting and burning-down process and may want to plan on serving this before a grilled main course, when the grill will be hot anyway. Use wood smoking chips for extra flavor, if you wish, or just grill the shrimp *al carbón.* Either way, the grilled shrimp are dipped into a fiery chipotle mayonnaise—a hot, pink, and smoky New Southwestern condiment that we just can't be without—or into a peppery garlic-lime mayonnaise, also a bad habit to acquire.

1 pound (about 24) medium shrimp, shelled and deveined
2 tablespoons olive oil
2 tablespoons fresh lime juice
2 garlic cloves, peeled and crushed through a press
½ teaspoon ground cumin
½ teaspoon salt

½ teaspoon freshly ground black pepper
1 cup mesquite or hickory wood smoking chips
Smoked Jalapeño-Lime Mayonnaise (page 23) or Peppery Garlic-Lime Mayonnaise (page 98), for dipping

In a nonreactive bowl, combine the shrimp, olive oil, lime juice, garlic, cumin, salt, and freshly ground pepper and let stand at room temperature, covered, for 1 hour, stirring once or twice.

Cover the wood chips with water and let them soak for at least 30 minutes.

Light a charcoal fire and let it burn down until the coals are evenly white or preheat a gas grill (medium heat).

Thread the shrimp onto metal skewers. Drain the wood chips and scatter them on the coals or over the grill stones. Position the rack about 6 inches above the heat source. Cover the grill and when the wood chips are smoking, lay the skewered shrimp on the rack. Cover and cook, turning the skewers once, until the shrimp are just cooked through, 2 to 3 minutes per side.

Remove the shrimp from the skewers and serve them hot, warm, or cool, accompanied by one of the mayonnaises for dipping.

serves 4 to 6

smoked jalapeño-lime mayonnaise

3 to 4 chipotles adobado, with
   clinging sauce
1 large egg, at room temperature
1 large egg yolk, at room
   temperature
2 tablespoons fresh lime juice

1 tablespoon minced lime zest
1 tablespoon prepared Dijon-style
   mustard
½ teaspoon salt
1 cup corn oil
½ cup olive oil

In a food processor, combine the chipotles, egg, egg yolk, lime juice, lime zest, mustard, and salt. Process until smooth. With the motor running, add the corn and olive oils through the feed tube in a quick, steady stream. The mayonnaise will thicken. Adjust the seasoning. Transfer to a storage container, cover, and refrigerate until use. *The mayonnaise can be prepared up to 3 days ahead.*

makes 2 cups

deep-fried stuffed jalapeños

These are small but very intensely flavored nibbles—which is, perhaps, the best possible definition of an appetizer worth eating. Don't scoff at the jalapeño–peanut butter combination until you've tried it, and don't blame us when you get hooked: The idea comes from Western cooking expert, restaurateur, and historian Sam Arnold.

24 large pickled jalapeño chiles
¼ cup Frijoles Refritos (page 179)
   or refried beans
¼ cup chunky peanut butter
4 ounces Monterey Jack cheese, cut
   into 8 ¼- by 1-inch strips
½ cup yellow cornmeal

½ cup unbleached all-purpose flour
½ teaspoon salt
2 eggs
Corn oil, for deep-frying
8 ounces sour cream, whisked until
   smooth and shiny, for dipping

Cut a short slit in the side of each jalapeño. Carefully scrape out as many seeds as possible but avoid tearing or enlarging the slit. Stuff each of 8 jalapeños with about 1 teaspoon of refried beans. Stuff 8 more jalapeños with about 1 teaspoon of peanut butter each. (The capacity of individual chiles will vary, but they should not be so full that the slits gape open.) Insert 1 strip of cheese into each of the 8 remaining chiles. On a plate, mix together the cornmeal, flour, and salt. In a small bowl, thoroughly whisk the eggs. One at a time, dip the jalapeños into the beaten egg and then roll them in the cornmeal mixture until well coated. Let the jalapeños stand on a rack for 30 minutes to firm the coating.

In a deep fryer or in a wide, deep pan fitted with a deep-fry thermometer, heat about 4 inches of corn oil (the fryer or pan should be no more than half full) to 375°F. Working in batches and using a slotted spoon, lower the jalapeños into the hot oil. Fry, turning the chiles gently, until they are just crisp and golden, about 4 minutes. (Overcooking the chiles may cause the fillings to boil away.)

With the slotted spoon, transfer the fried jalapeños to absorbent paper. Keep the chiles warm in a 250° F oven until all have been fried. Serve them hot or warm, accompanied by sour cream for dipping.

makes 24, serving 6 to 8

nachos

These Tex-Mex snacks too would be at home in the tortilla chapter, but they are such a popular appetizer and snack we decided to put them here. In El Paso (where it's said they were invented) they're found on the menus of all manner of eateries from authentic Mexican to fast-food chains, and they turn up in home kitchens just as frequently. They're one of our favorite quick and easy accompaniments to margaritas or beers. Here is a traditional recipe, followed by two variations.

classic nachos

These are nachos just like Mom used to make—if Mom ran a west Texas cantina. Actually the tomatoes and green onions are atypical embellishments, but colorful and tasty ones. Substitute homemade refried black beans for added flair and serve the nachos as is, or offer Mantequilla de los Pobres (page 11) or smooth, cool sour cream to dip them in.

36 Tostaditas (page 32) or unspiced, lightly salted, commercially prepared corn tortilla chips
¾ cup Frijoles Refritos (page 179)
4 to 6 large pickled jalapeño chiles, stemmed and sliced into thin rounds
4 plum tomatoes (about ¾ pound), juiced, seeded, and diced

2 green onions, trimmed and sliced (about ⅓ cup)
¾ cup (about 3 ounces) grated Monterey Jack cheese
¾ cup (about 3 ounces) grated medium-sharp cheddar cheese

Position a rack in the upper third of the oven and preheat the oven to 475°F.

Spread each tostadita with about 1 teaspoon of the frijoles refritos and arrange them in a single layer in a large shallow, heat-proof serving dish. Scatter the jalapeños, tomatoes, and green onions over the beans. Sprinkle with the cheeses and bake about 5 minutes, or until the cheeses are melted and the nachos are sizzling and lightly browned. Serve immediately.

serves 4 to 6

chili parlor nachos

Eating these nachos—mounded high, mortared together with melted cheese, and napped with steaming chili con carne—is an exercise in manual dexterity and greed: Provide plenty of napkins. In Texas there are some pretty good brands of canned chili for sale, but in the rest of the country you may prefer to use homemade.

½ recipe Tostaditas (page 32) or 8
ounces unspiced, lightly salted,
commercially prepared tortilla
chips
2½ cups (about 10 ounces) grated
medium-sharp cheddar cheese
6 pickled jalapeño chiles, stemmed
and minced

1½ cups chili with beans
1 medium onion, peeled and diced
(about 1 cup)
4 ounces sour cream, whisked until
smooth and shiny

Position a rack in the upper third of the oven and preheat the oven to 425°F.

Layer half of the tostaditas in a round 10-inch ovenproof serving dish (we use a white ceramic quiche dish). Scatter half the cheese and half the jalapeños evenly over the tostaditas. Mound the remaining tostaditas in the dish. Scatter the remaining cheese and jalapeños over these tostaditas. Bake 10 to 12 minutes, or until the cheese is melted and the tostaditas are lightly browned.

Meanwhile, in a small saucepan over medium heat, bring the chili to a simmer, stirring occasionally. Pour the chili evenly over the hot nachos. Sprinkle the onions evenly over the chili, top the entire business with the sour cream, and serve immediately.

serves 4 to 6

blue corn nachos with
bacon and sweet onions

Sweet Vidalia-type onions are grown throughout the El Paso area, and their abundance inspired these nontraditional but otherwise delicious nachos. Prepared with extra-corny-tasting blue tostaditas and dipped into palate-cooling sour cream, they're an improvisation that's become a kitchen favorite. When possible we use mesquite-smoked bacon, but the regular supermarket sort also makes good eating.

½ pound sliced bacon
36 Tostaditas (page 32) or unspiced, lightly salted, commercially prepared corn tortilla chips
1 medium sweet onion, peeled and finely diced (about 1 cup)
6 pickled jalapeño chiles, stemmed and minced

2 cups (about 8 ounces) grated Monterey Jack cheese or mozzarella cheese or a combination of both
8 ounces sour cream, whisked until smooth, for dipping

ᐤᐤᐤᐤᐤᐤᐤᐤᐤᐤᐤᐤ

Position a rack in the upper third of the oven and preheat the oven to 475°F.

Spread the bacon slices in a large skillet. Set over medium heat and cook, turning once or twice, until crisp, 8 to 10 minutes. Drain on absorbent paper. When the bacon is cool, coarsely chop it.

Arrange the tostaditas in a single layer in a large shallow heat-proof serving dish. Scatter the bacon, onions, and jalapeños evenly over the tostaditas. Sprinkle the cheese evenly over all. Bake about 5 minutes, or until the cheese is melted and the nachos are sizzling and lightly browned. Serve them immediately, accompanied by the sour cream, for dipping.

serves 4 to 6

an enchilada dinner

Classic 1-1-1 Margaritas (page 238)

Salsa del Norte (page 4) and Mantequilla de los Pobres (page 11)
with Tostaditas (page 32) and Chicharrones

Enchiladas de las Colonias (page 36)
Texmati Pilaf (page 181)
Frijoles Refritos (page 179)

Forti's Almond Flan (page 234)

chapter two

the tortilla kitchen
southwestern staples based on corn and flour tortillas

In El Paso a recent restaurant survey named the hamburger the most commonly enjoyed restaurant meal, an ominous fact that nevertheless says more about the ubiquity of the likes of McDonald's than it does about any erosion of Southwestern traditions. *Hamburguesas al carbón* may well win a single-dish survey, but buns will never replace tortillas, and dishes based upon specially treated ground corn, corn tortillas, and (to a lesser extent) flour tortillas, remain fundamental to most meals, home-prepared or in a restaurant. In El Paso it's not uncommon to find a supermarket with its own tortilla section turning out warm fresh tortillas right next to a big display of cold factory-made hamburger buns. We like that.

tostaditas

Tostaditas are corn tortilla chips, but they are *not* Doritos and they are *not* Fritos. The former are a snack food (frequently seasoned with an acrid spice mixture), the latter are a Texas institution (and we love 'em), but crisp, light, home-fried chips made from real corn tortillas are quite another thing altogether. The difference between extruded, batter-based snack chips and genuine tostaditas made from fresh tortillas is like the difference between a Pringle and a homemade potato chip. The difference between store-bought tostaditas and those freshly fried is also substantial, and unless you have access to an excellent packaged brand, we encourage you to get into the habit of making your own (in fact, El Paso area restaurants, especially those north of town that are of New Mexican origin, regularly serve warm, fresh tostaditas). You needn't use homemade tortillas to get great results, by the way, and you may find that the quantity produced by this recipe serves far fewer than eight—they're that good.

24 6-inch yellow or blue corn tortillas	About 2 teaspoons salt
4 cups (about) corn oil, for deep-frying	

Stack several tortillas together, and with a long sharp knife, cut them into 6 equal wedges. Repeat with the remaining tortillas. If the tortillas are fresh, spread them in a layer on the counter and let them dry out for about 1 hour (excess moisture can cause splattering during deep-frying).

In a deep fryer or in a deep, heavy pot fitted with a deep-fry thermometer, heat about 4 inches of the corn oil to between 375°F and 400°F. (The oil should come no more than halfway up the side of the fryer.) Working in batches to avoid crowding the fryer, cook the tostaditas, stirring once or twice, for about 1 minute or until they are crisp but not browned. With a slotted spoon, transfer the tostaditas to absorbent paper. Sprinkle them lightly with salt to taste. Repeat the frying and salting with the remaining tostaditas. The tostaditas can be stored, airtight, for up to 1 day. Rewarm them, wrapped in a paper bag, in a 200°F oven for about 10 minutes.

serves 8 or fewer

enchiladas de santa fe
(flat cheese enchiladas with red chile pod sauce)

These flat (stacked, not rolled) enchiladas, filled with cheese and napped with a rich sauce made of soaked and puréed dried red chile pods, are what we think of as the quintessential enchiladas—the best and purest example of a rather large and frisky genre. You may serve each stack *con huevo* (topped with a sunny-side up egg) if you wish. The blending of fiery sauce and bland yolk is wonderful, particularly for brunch or breakfast. Park dislikes crunchy lettuce garnishes, but Norma finds that most people welcome the contrasting texture and temperature of a fistful of shredded romaine beside their enchiladas.

About 1 cup corn oil
12 6-inch corn tortillas
Red Chile Pod Sauce (page 34)
12 ounces (about 3 cups) shredded
    Monterey Jack cheese or medium-
    sharp cheddar cheese or a combi-
    nation of both

½ cup minced onion
3 green onions, trimmed and sliced
    (about ⅓ cup), for garnish
2 cups shredded romaine, for
    garnish

Position a rack in the middle of the oven and preheat the oven to 375°F.

In a medium skillet, warm ½ inch of corn oil over moderate heat. Using tongs, dip the tortillas one at a time into the oil, turn them, and then transfer them to absorbent paper. The tortillas should be in the oil no more than a few seconds, and the oil should be hot enough to soften the tortillas but not so hot that the edges begin to crisp.

In a second skillet over low heat, warm the red chile pod sauce until it simmers. Spread about ½ cup of the sauce in the bottom of a shallow baking dish large enough to hold 4 corn tortillas in a single, nonoverlapping layer. (Or use 4 individual, heat-proof round gratin dishes.)

Using tongs, one at a time, turn 4 of the tortillas in the hot sauce (they should be no more than lightly coated, and if the sauce seems too thick, thin it with a bit of chicken broth). Transfer the dipped tortillas to the baking dish, arranging them in a single layer. Sprinkle about ¼ cup of the cheese and about 1 tablespoon of the white onions evenly over each tortilla. Repeat the dipping process with 4 more tortillas, stacking each on top of one of the cheese-topped tortillas. Sprinkle about ¼ cup of the cheese and about 1 tablespoon of the white onions over the second layer of tortillas. Dip the last 4 tortillas in the sauce and place one on top of each of the stacks in the dish. Pour any sauce remaining in the skillet evenly over the enchilada stacks and sprinkle them evenly with the remaining cheese.

Bake 10 to 12 minutes, or until the cheese is melted, the sauce is bubbling, and the enchiladas are heated through. With a wide spatula, transfer each enchilada stack to a heated plate. Sprinkle with green onions, garnish with romaine, and serve immediately.

serves 4

red chile pod sauce

The red chile pods used in this sauce are the same that form the long hanging strings (*ristras*) and wreaths that are a tourist's best souvenir of a trip to the Southwest. Be certain your *ristra* has not been coated with varnish (which discourages insects but renders the pods inedible), and you can then simply snip off as many chiles as you need, having your souvenir and eating it too. Time can be saved by substituting 2¼ cups homemade or purchased frozen or jarred chile purée (page 250), and although to our palates the flavor will not be quite as wonderful, the convenience is undeniable.

½ pound (about 24) large dried red New Mexico chile pods

2 to 3 chiles de arbol

3 cups water

3 tablespoons olive oil

½ cup minced onion

2 garlic cloves, peeled and minced

¾ teaspoon ground cumin

¾ teaspoon dried oregano, crumbled

2 tablespoons unbleached all-purpose flour

1¼ cups chicken broth, homemade or canned

1½ teaspoons salt

1½ teaspoons cider vinegar

¾ teaspoon packed light brown sugar

Stem the chile pods and the chiles de arbol and slit them open (kitchen scissors work well here). Shake out as many of the seeds as possible and rinse the chiles briefly under cold running water. Tear or snip them into 1-inch pieces.

Bring the water to a boil and pour it over the chile pieces in a medium heat-proof bowl. Cover the bowl with a pot lid or a plate and let the chile pieces stand, stirring them once or twice, until the water is cool.

With a slotted spoon, transfer the softened chile pieces to the jar of a blender or the workbowl of a food processor. Process briefly, scraping down the sides. Add some of the soaking water and process again. Continue adding water, blending, and then scraping down the sides until the water has all been used and the chile purée is smooth. Transfer the purée to a strainer set over a bowl. Add 2 tablespoons hot tap water to the blender and purée briefly to rinse the blades and the inside. Add this residue to the purée in the strainer. Force the chile purée through the strainer with a stiff rubber spatula, discarding any seeds and tough bits of peel remaining in the strainer. *The purée can be stored, well covered, in the refrigerator for up to 3 days, or frozen for up to 1 month.*

In a medium saucepan over low heat, warm the olive oil. Add the onions, garlic, cumin, and oregano and cook, uncovered, stirring often, for 5 minutes. Whisk in the flour and cook, stirring and mashing the flour mixture, for 2 minutes. Whisk in the chile pod purée, chicken broth, salt, cider vinegar, and brown sugar. Bring to a boil, then lower the heat and simmer, partially covered, stirring once or twice, for 20 minutes, or until the sauce has thickened. Adjust the seasoning (to best appreciate the completed sauce, sample it on a piece of tortilla or bread). Remove from the heat, cool to room temperature, and transfer to a storage container. *The sauce can be prepared up to 2 days ahead and refrigerated, or frozen for up to 1 month.*

makes about 3¼ cups

santa fe supper

Chilled Dos Equis Beer

Blue Corn Nachos with Bacon and Sweet Onions (page 28)

Enchiladas de Santa Fe (page 33) con Huevo
Pico de Gallo (page 3)

Sopaipillas (page 223)

---

enchiladas de las colonias
(chicken enchiladas with pueblo-styled mole sauce)

These colonial-style enchiladas probably began as a sensible way to use up leftover sauce and turkey from the great Mexican dish *mole poblano de guajolote*—turkey in a dark and spicy sauce from Pueblo. (Yes, the sauce includes chocolate—a bit—but it includes many other things as well, and the resulting flavor is deeply complex and only slightly sweet.) The enchiladas de la colonias that appear on most El Paso and Juárez restaurant menus are made with chicken and with bottled sauce (the turkey dish itself is fairly rare) and local cooks know plenty of ways to doctor up the latter for maximum authentic flavor. (Not all bottled mole poblano pastes are clearly labeled, by the way. The two most commonly found brands are Doña Maria and Rogelio Bueno. The product needed for this recipe—however it is labeled—is packed in a small jar resembling a juice glass, is a rich, ruddy brown, and among its listed ingredients you will find sesame seeds, various chiles, and chocolate.) From "Big Virginia" Lopez, the original owner of The Hacienda, one of our favorite restaurants, we picked up the tip of adding a bit of peanut butter to the sauce and of garnishing the enchiladas with sesame seeds. Our own truc is to combine two different brands of bottled mole to achieve the maximum complexity of flavor. When you're feeling adventurous, you might also consider Park's saucy additions of a dollop of orange marmalade and/or a grating of Mexican chocolate. The dish is rich—serve it with refried black or pinto beans, generously sprinkled with sharp feta cheese, and plenty of warm flour tortillas.

1½ tablespoons sesame seeds

2 jars (approximately 8¾ ounces each) prepared mole poblano paste

¼ cup peanut butter

About 3½ cups chicken broth, homemade or canned

About 1½ cups corn oil

12 6-inch corn tortillas

4 cups Pollo Deshebrada (page 147)

About 2 teaspoons salt

¾ cup minced onion

10 ounces (about 2½ cups) grated Monterey Jack cheese or mozzarella cheese or a combination of both

1 cup Crema (page 254) or crème fraîche

Position a rack in the upper third of the oven and preheat the oven to 375°F.

In a small heavy skillet over low heat, toast the sesame seeds, stirring them occasionally, until they are golden, about 5 minutes. Remove them immediately from the skillet.

In a medium heavy skillet over low heat, combine the mole poblano paste and peanut butter. Cook, mashing and stirring often, until almost melted. Gradually whisk in enough chicken broth to make a smooth, medium-thick sauce.

Meanwhile, in a deep skillet, warm about ½ inch of corn oil over medium heat. Using tongs, dip the tortillas one at a time into the oil, turn them, and then transfer them to absorbent paper. The tortillas should be in the oil no more than a few seconds, and the oil should be hot enough to soften the tortillas but not so hot that the edges begin to crisp.

Spread about ¾ cup of the mole sauce in the bottom of a large shallow baking dish. (It can be any shape, but it should be a size to just comfortably hold 12 rolled and filled enchiladas. The standard 9-by 13-inch pan is a bit too small.) Or use 4 individual heat-proof serving dishes.

Using tongs, dip a tortilla into the hot mole sauce. Let some of the excess drip off, then lay the tortilla on a plate. Spread about ⅓ cup of the shredded chicken across the lower third of the tortilla. Season the meat lightly with salt, sprinkle it with about 1 tablespoon of the onions, and top it with about 2½ tablespoons grated cheese. Roll the enchilada and lay it, seam-side down, in the baking dish. Repeat with the remaining tortillas, chicken, onions, leaving about ½ cup of the grated cheese. Drizzle ¾ cup of mole sauce evenly over the enchiladas and sprinkle them with the remaining cheese.

Loosely cover the dish with foil and bake about 12 minutes, or until the enchiladas are heated through and the sauce is bubbling. With a wide spatula, transfer the enchiladas to heated plates. Spoon a generous ribbon of crema down the center of each portion. Sprinkle the sesame seeds over all, and serve immediately.

serves 4

enchiladas de pollo verdes
(cheese and chicken enchiladas with
tomatillo–green chile sauce)

These are for enchilada connoisseurs. Those who find red chile enchiladas "too plain" and enchiladas de a colonias "too rich" delight in this tart green sauce that combines roasted chopped chiles and tomatillos. The enchiladas can be filled with cheese alone, but we prefer the combination of cheese and shredded chicken. For creamy *enchiladas suizas* (Swiss style), replace ½ cup of the chicken broth with ½ cup Crema (page 254) or crème fraîche.

7 long green chiles
2½ teaspoons salt
1 pound (about 12 medium) tomatillos
1¼ cups finely chopped onion
2 or 3 fresh jalapeño chiles, stemmed and chopped
2 garlic cloves, peeled and chopped
About 1½ cups chicken broth, homemade or canned

2 tablespoons olive oil
About 1½ cups corn oil
12 6-inch corn tortillas
4 cups Pollo Deshebrada (page 147)
3 cups (about 12 ounces) Monterey Jack cheese or medium-sharp cheddar cheese or a combination of both
2 cups shredded romaine, for garnish

In the open flame of a gas burner or under a preheated broiler, roast the long green chiles, turning them, until they are lightly but evenly charred. Steam the chiles in a paper bag, or in a bowl, covered with a plate, until cool. Rub away the burned peel. Stem and seed the chiles and coarsely chop them. There should be about 1 cup.

Position a rack in the upper third of the oven and preheat the oven to 375°F.

Bring a saucepan of water to a boil. Stir in 1 teaspoon salt, add the tomatillos, and cook them about 10 minutes or until they are very tender. Drain and cool them to room temperature.

In a blender, combine the tomatillos, ½ cup of the onions, the jalapeños, garlic, and 1½ teaspoons salt. Blend until smooth. In a 4-cup measure, combine the tomatillo purée and chopped green chiles. Add enough chicken broth to equal 4 cups. In a medium skillet over moderate heat, warm the olive oil. When it is very hot, add the tomatillo mixture (it may spatter), lower the heat, and cook, stirring occasionally, for 10 minutes.

In a deep skillet, warm about ½ inch of corn oil over medium heat. Using tongs, immerse the tortillas one at a time in the oil, turn them, and then transfer them to absorbent paper. The tortillas should be in the oil no more than a few seconds, and the oil should be hot enough to soften the tortillas but not so hot that the edges begin to crisp.

Spread about ¾ cup of the tomatillo sauce in the bottom of a large shallow baking dish. (It can be any shape, but it should be a size to just comfortably hold 12 rolled and filled enchiladas. The standard 9- by 13-inch pan is a bit too small.) Or use 4 individual heat-proof serving dishes.

Using tongs, dip a tortilla into the tomatillo sauce, then lay the tortilla on a plate. Spread about ⅓ cup pollo deshebrada across the lower third of the tortilla. Season the meat lightly with salt, sprinkle it with about 1 tablespoon of the remaining onions, and top it with about 2½ tablespoons grated cheese. Roll the enchilada and lay it, seam-side down, in the baking dish. Repeat with the remaining tortillas, chicken, onions, leaving about ¾ cup of the grated cheese. Drizzle the remaining sauce evenly over the enchiladas and sprinkle them with the remaining cheese.

Bake 12 minutes, or until the enchiladas are heated through, the cheese is melted, and the sauce is bubbling. With a wide spatula, transfer the enchiladas from the large baking dish to heated plates, garnish them with shredded romaine, and serve immediately.

serves 4

green enchiladas "the hacienda"

Generations of El Pasoans have enjoyed the food at The Hacienda, a comfortable, casual restaurant that assumes the role of a home away from home for many of us. Over the years there Park and his sister Monica have celebrated everything from good report cards in grade school to Christmas vacations home from college to successful important business deals. The food is simple but good, and none of it is more delicious than the green enchiladas filled with cheese and chicken and topped with a sauce thickly tangled with strips of roasted green chiles. Fiery, cheesey, and multitextured, they are Park's absolute favorite enchiladas. Here is our modest attempt, for those who will never get to The Hacienda, to duplicate them.

9 long green chiles
2 tablespoons olive oil
1¼ cups finely chopped onion
2 garlic cloves, peeled and minced
½ teaspoon dried oregano, crumbled
1½ cups chicken broth, homemade or canned
1¼ cups canned crushed tomatoes with added purée

Salt
About 1½ cups corn oil
12 6-inch corn tortillas
4 cups Pollo Deshebrada (page 147)
3 cups (about 12 ounces) grated Monterey Jack cheese or medium-sharp cheddar cheese or a combination of both
2 cups shredded romaine, for garnish

In the open flame of a gas burner or under a preheated broiler, roast the long green chiles, turning them, until they are lightly but evenly charred. Steam the chiles in a paper bag, or in a bowl, covered with a plate, until cool. Rub away the burned peel. Stem and seed the chiles and cut them into ¼-inch-wide strips.

Position a rack in the upper third of the oven and preheat the oven to 375°F.

In a medium saucepan over low heat, warm the olive oil. Add ½ cup of the onions, the garlic, and oregano and cook, covered, stirring once or twice, for 10 minutes. Stir in the chicken broth and tomatoes. Chop enough of the chile strips to equal ½ cup. Add both the chopped and whole chiles to the saucepan, stir in 1 teaspoon salt, and bring to a boil. Lower the heat, partially cover, and simmer, stirring once or twice, for 10 minutes. Adjust the seasoning.

In a deep skillet, warm about ½ inch of corn oil over medium heat. Using tongs, immerse the tortillas one at a time in the oil, turn them, and then transfer them to absorbent paper. The tortillas should be in the oil no more than a few seconds, and the oil should be hot enough to soften the tortillas but not so hot that the edges begin to crisp.

Spread about ¾ cup of the sauce in the bottom of a large shallow baking dish. (It can be any shape, but it should be a size to just comfortably hold 12 rolled and filled enchiladas. The standard 9- by 13-inch pan is a bit too small.) Or use 4 individual heat-proof serving dishes.

Using tongs, dip a tortilla into the hot sauce, then lay the tortilla on a plate. Spread about ⅓ cup pollo deshebrada across the lower third of the tortilla. Season the meat lightly with salt, sprinkle it with about 1 tablespoon of the remaining onions, and top it with about 2½ tablespoons grated cheese. Roll the enchilada and lay it, seam-side down, in the baking dish. Repeat with the remaining tortillas, chicken, onions, leaving about ¾ cup of the grated cheese. Drizzle the remaining sauce evenly over the enchiladas and sprinkle them with the remaining cheese.

Bake 12 minutes, or until the enchiladas are heated through, the cheese is melted, and the sauce is bubbling. With a wide spatula, transfer the enchiladas from the large baking dish to heated plates, garnish them with shredded romaine, and serve immediately.

serves 4

beef tacos al carbón

Cooking *al carbón*—grilling over charcoal, especially beef—is a great speciality of northern Mexico, and thus, by extension, of El Paso. One of the best ways to appreciate the rather chewy cuts preferred by Mexican cooks is in tacos *al carbón*, for which the meat, after being marinated and grilled, is coarsely diced and then folded into warmed corn tortillas along with guacamole, salsa, and a grilled green onion—the standard edible garnish for this dish. (When you eat these tacos you will see, we think, where the general inspiration for fajitas came from.) In restaurants the meat is often reheated and dry (it's just not something that can be successfully prepared to order for a single diner), but at home, cooked for a crowd, the steak comes juicy and hot off the grill and the tacos are sublime. For chicken tacos al carbón, substitute the grilled marinated chicken breast from the pasta salad recipe on page 149.

½ cup fresh lime juice
3 tablespoons olive oil plus additional oil for grilling the green onions
2 garlic cloves, peeled and crushed through a press
1 teaspoon salt
½ teaspoon freshly ground black pepper
1½ pounds flank steak, trimmed of external fat

16 large green onions, trimmed (leave no more than 3 inches of green top)
16 6-inch corn tortillas, warmed
Guacamole (page 10) or Mantequilla de los Pobres (page 11)
Pico de Gallo (page 3) or Salsa del Norte (page 4)

In a shallow nonreactive dish, stir together the lime juice, 3 tablespoons olive oil, garlic, salt, and freshly ground pepper. Add the flank steak and let it stand at room temperature, covered, turning it once or twice, for 4 hours.

Preheat a gas grill (medium high) or light a charcoal fire and let it burn down until the coals are evenly white. Adjust the rack to 6 inches above the heat source. Lay the flank steak on the rack and grill it, covered, turning the steak once, for a total of about 12 minutes for medium-rare, or until done to your liking. Transfer the steak to a cutting board, tent it with foil, and let stand for 10 minutes.

Brush the green onions lightly with olive oil and lay them on the grill rack. Cover and cook, turning them once, until they are just lightly browned and becoming tender, a total of 3 to 4 minutes. Transfer them to a platter.

Carve the flank steak across the grain and at a slight angle into ½-inch slices. Cut the slices crosswise into ½-inch cubes. Serve immediately, accompanied by the grilled onions, tortillas, guacamole, and salsa.

16 tacos, serving 4 to 6

a grill supper

White Sangria (page 241)

Grilled Shrimp Quesadillas (page 19)
Queso Fundido on the Grill (page 20) and Salsa del Norte (page 4) with
Tostaditas (page 32)

Beef Tacos al Carbón (page 42)
Ensalada de Nopalitos (page 202)
Texas Three-Bean Salad (page 200)

Mango-Peach Ice Cream with Dulce Crunch (page 230)

red pork street tacos

Tacos, like enchiladas, come in all forms, and though El Paso serves up plenty of the crisp, ground-beef-filled Tex-Mex restaurant kind, when the Kerrs get a taco craving we turn instead to this recipe. It is our attempt to re-create the street tacos sold by sidewalk vendors in Mexico City and elsewhere. It's a more informal taco, primitive and messy (but aren't they all?); and though you can tuck in a bit of lettuce, cheese, tomato, and salsa if you want, the fundamental flavors and textures of moist pork, rich red chile, and slightly chewy corn tortilla render such adornments unnecessary.

3 cups Pork Deshebrada (page 130)
1½ cups braising liquid from the
    Pork Deshebrada

¾ cup finely minced onion
About 1½ cups corn oil
12 6-inch corn tortillas

In a small saucepan over medium heat, combine the pork deshebrada and the braising liquid. Bring to a brisk simmer and cook, uncovered, stirring often, until the liquid has reduced and just coats the meat, about 7 minutes. Remove the pork from the heat and stir in the onions.

In a large skillet, warm about ½ inch of corn oil over medium heat. Spread 1/12 of the pork mixture across the center of 1 corn tortilla and fold it in half. With the aid of a pancake turner, lower the taco into the hot oil. Hold it closed with the spatula until the tortilla has firmed enough to stay closed on its own. Repeat this with the rest of the pork mixture and tortillas, working in batches if necessary. Fry the tacos, turning them once, until they are crisp/chewy (the tortillas should not become hard), about 2 minutes per side. Transfer them to absorbent paper. The tacos can be kept warm in a 200°F oven for up to 20 minutes if necessary.

makes 12 tacos

chicken flautas

Flautas are flutes—corn tortillas formed into tubes around a shredded chicken filling and fried crisp. The most typical local preparation is made with half a tortilla, tightly rolled to cigarette-size dimensions, but at Forti's Mexican Elder (one of our favorite restaurants) and elsewhere, flautas have gotten larger. Prepared with a whole corn tortilla filled and rolled into a 1-inch cylinder, these flautas are then fried to a state somewhere short of totally crisp. The change in proportion of chicken to tortilla and the slightly chewier texture make two or three of these larger flutes a satisfying meal and we cook them often. (The skinny version still has its place in our kitchen, prepared as an easy-to-pass, easy-to-eat cocktail finger food.)

12 6-inch corn tortillas	Avocado Sauce (page 46) and Salsa
4 cups Pollo Deshebrada (page 147)	del Norte (page 4) or
Salt	Crema (page 254) and Santos's Salsa
About 2 cups corn oil	Verde (page 6)
4 cups finely shredded romaine	

Lay a corn tortilla on the work surface. Arrange about ⅓ cup of pollo deshebrada across the lower third of the tortilla. Season the meat with a pinch of salt and roll the tortilla into a tube about 1 inch in diameter. Secure with a toothpick. Repeat this to make the rest of the flautas. *The flautas can be filled up to 1 hour ahead. Wrap them well and store at room temperature.*

In a large deep skillet, warm about ½ inch of corn oil over medium heat. Add the flautas, working in batches if necessary, and fry, turning them once, until they are almost (but not quite) crisp, about 2 minutes per side. With tongs, transfer the flautas to absorbent paper to drain.

Make a thin layer of shredded romaine on 4 to 6 plates. Arrange 2 or 3 flautas on top of the romaine. Spoon a ribbon of avocado sauce or crema across the flautas and serve them immediately, accompanied by salsa del norte or Santos's salsa verde.

serves 4 to 6

avocado sauce

This smooth, pale green, and slightly tart avocado sauce is traditionally ribboned over Chicken Flautas (page 45) but it is also good over plain grilled chicken, shrimp, or fish steaks.

1 buttery-ripe black-skinned avo-
    cado, pitted and peeled
¾ cup sour cream

2 tablespoons lime juice
½ teaspoon salt

In a small food processor, combine the avocado, sour cream, lime juice, and salt and process, stopping once or twice to scrape down the sides of the bowl, until very smooth. Adjust the seasoning. Transfer to a storage container and cover with plastic wrap, pressing the film onto the surface of the sauce. *The sauce can be prepared up to 6 hours ahead.*

makes about 1½ cups

tostadas compuestas

You know you're heading toward New Mexico when these crisp-fried corn tortilla cups, filled with rich red pork chili and topped with cheese, lettuce, and tomatoes, make a menu appearance. The only drawback to cooking them at home is finding the basket for frying the tortillas. We've tried various methods of producing the cups (some quite cumbersome and downright dangerous) but have never been satisfied that they looked as good (or held the requisite amount of chili) as they do at places like Grigg's. We don't even have a regular source for the baskets (which consist of two open wire cups, one slightly smaller than the other, each on a long handle, and meant to nest together with the tortilla in between), though we have seen them in the past in such catalogs as Williams-Sonoma, which is where we acquired ours some years ago. Trust us, the search is worth it.

Corn oil, for deep-frying
12 6-inch corn tortillas
About 1½ teaspoons salt
3 cups Corona Ranch Chili con
  Carne Colorado (page 69)
3 cups shredded romaine
3 cups (about 12 ounces) grated
  medium-sharp cheddar cheese

2 medium tomatoes (about 1
  pound), cored, seeded, and
  chopped
Salsa del Norte (page 4) or Pico de
  Gallo (page 3)

In a deep fryer or in a deep heavy pan fitted with a frying thermometer, heat about 6 inches of oil (the deep fryer should be no more than half full) to between 375°F and 400°F. Dip both cups of a corn-tortilla-frying basket into the oil. Place a tortilla between the cups, fit them together, lower the tortilla into the hot oil, and fry about 1 minute, or until crisp. Carefully remove the tortilla shell from the basket and transfer it to absorbent paper. Season it lightly with salt. Repeat this to make the rest of the tortilla shells. *The tortilla shells can be prepared up to 1 day ahead. Store them, airtight, at room temperature. Warm the shells before using them in a paper bag in a 200°F oven.*

In a medium saucepan over low heat, bring the chili to a simmer, stirring often. Set 2 or 3 tortilla shells on each of 4 to 6 plates. Spoon the chili into the shells, filling them about halfway. Top the chili with romaine, cheese, and tomatoes and serve immediately, passing salsa at the table.

serves 4 to 6

gorditas
(beef-filled fried masa turnovers)

These "little fat ones" (as the name translates) began as thickish soft padlike masa tortillas topped with beans, cheese, lettuce, salsa, etc. In certain El Paso restaurants the masa tortillas have gotten thicker, so thick that even after frying the masa inside remains raw and has to be scooped out and discarded. Then what has become a crisp cornmeal turnover is filled with a mild but savory mixture of ground meat and diced potato. The garnishes—shredded lettuce, grated cheese, sweet juicy tomatoes, and potent salsa—lift the whole business into the realm of the best cheeseburger/taco hybrid you'll ever eat. Fanatics can easily put away three gorditas, but in order to avoid becoming little fat ones ourselves we try to stop at two.

FILLING

1 large (½ pound) boiling potato, peeled
¼ teaspoon salt
2 tablespoons olive oil
½ cup finely diced onion

1 garlic clove, peeled and minced
¼ teaspoon chili powder blend
¼ teaspoon ground cumin
¼ teaspoon dried oregano
¾ pound lean ground beef

DOUGH

2 cups masa harina de maiz (page 253)
¼ cup unbleached all-purpose flour
1 teaspoon baking powder
½ teaspoon salt
½ teaspoon freshly ground black pepper
3 tablespoons lard
1¼ cups hot tap water

Corn oil, for deep-frying
⅔ cup shredded romaine
⅔ cup grated medium-sharp cheddar cheese
½ cup diced ripe tomato
Salsa del Norte (page 4) or Pico de Gallo (page 3) or a good-quality tomato-based bottled hot salsa

FOR THE FILLING

In a medium saucepan, cover the potato with cold water. Stir in 2 teaspoons salt, set over medium heat, and bring to a boil. Lower the heat slightly and cook until the potato is just tender, about 20 minutes. Drain, cool the potato completely, and cut it into ¼-inch dice.

In a medium skillet over low heat, warm the olive oil. Stir in the onions, garlic, chili powder blend, cumin, and oregano and cook, partially covered, for 5 minutes. Add the meat, crumbling it thoroughly, stir in ¼ teaspoon salt, and cook uncovered, stirring occasionally, until the meat is cooked through, about 12 minutes. Stir in the diced potato and adjust the seasoning. *The filling can be prepared 1 day ahead. Warm it up over low heat, stirring often.*

FOR THE DOUGH

In a food processor, combine the masa, flour, baking powder, salt, and freshly ground pepper and pulse to blend. Add the lard and process to form a crumbly dough. Add the water and process to form a smooth, moist dough. Transfer the dough to a bowl, cover it, and let it stand at room temperature for 30 minutes.

Divide the dough into 8 equal portions. Shape each portion into a disk about 2½ inches in diameter and about ½-inch thick.

TO ASSEMBLE

In a deep fryer or in a wide deep pan fitted with a deep-fry thermometer, heat about 4 inches of corn oil (the fryer or pan should be no more than half full) to 375°F. Working in batches, lower the gorditas into the hot oil and cook them, turning them once or twice, until they are crisp and lightly browned, about 4 minutes. With a slotted spoon transfer them to absorbent paper.

Holding the hot gorditas one at a time in a pot holder, with a serrated table knife, cut a slit halfway around the circumference of each one. Squeeze gently to open the slit and scrape out all the uncooked dough inside.

Spoon the meat mixture into the masa shells, filling them about ⅔ full. Fill the rest of the gorditas with the romaine, cheese, and tomatoes and serve them immediately, accompanied by the salsa.

serves 4

red pork tamales

Among the most ancient of New World foods, tamales are eaten widely throughout South and Central America and consist of a savory filling enclosed in a corn dough and wrapped in corn husks then steamed (though versions ranging from traditional to new wave also use such varied fillings and wrappers as lobster and banana leaves). Tamales are thought to be a lot of work, but from the recipe here you'll see that the ingredient list is short and it's mostly a mechanical matter of spreading and folding. This is the kind of kitchen process that quickly becomes second nature, and at Christmastime, when tamales are traditionally enjoyed in abundance, a tamale-making session, with a number of good friends chatting and sharing the work load, is an easygoing way to produce the dozens and dozens of tamales necessary for a proper party. (The rest of the year most El Pasoans buy their tamales from a good source or enjoy them in restaurants only.) To get you started, we have written the recipe for a relatively modest amount of basic red pork tamales, but you'll quickly graduate to quantity production if you like them as much as we do. These can be enjoyed as is, served hot in their steamy corn husks which you unfold to get at the moist, savory dumpling within. Or, you may pass heated Red Chile Pod Sauce (page 34) at the table for ad hoc application. Or, for a more complex, restaurant-style presentation, you may arrange opened tamales on individual heat-proof plates, nap them with Red Chile Pod Sauce, top them with grated Monterey Jack cheese, and bake them until all is hot and bubbling. Note that you'll need a deep pot into which a large-size vegetable steamer or stainless steel colander will fit. Tamales freeze well for up to 1 month and can be reheated in a microwave oven or in a double boiler or steamer.

6 cups Pork Deshebrada (page 130)	1 cup lard, at room temperature
6 cups braising liquid from the pork	1½ cups chicken broth, homemade
5 cups masa harina de maiz	or canned
1 tablespoon baking powder	2 3-ounce packages dried corn husk
1½ teaspoons salt	wrappers for tamales (hojas)

In a medium saucepan over moderate heat, combine the shredded pork and 4½ cups of the braising liquid. Bring to a simmer and cook, uncovered, stirring once or twice, for about 10 minutes, or until the liquid is reduced by half. The pork mixture should be moist and saucy, but not sloppily wet. Cool to room temperature. *The filling can be prepared up to 1 day ahead.*

In a food processor, combine the masa harina de maiz, baking powder, and salt and process to blend. Add the lard, chicken broth, and remaining braising liquid and process until a smooth dough is formed. Transfer to bowl, cover, and let stand at room temperature for 30 minutes.

Separate the corn husks and rinse them under running water to remove any clinging silks. Discard any husks that are undersized or torn; you should have about 30 usable husks. Soak them in a large bowl of cold water until flexible, about 20 minutes.

Shake the moisture off a corn husk and lay it on the work surface, pointed end away from you. Spread the wider two thirds of the husk with an even layer of the masa dough about ¼-inch thick. Place about ¼ cup of the meat filling longways in the center of the masa. Fold in one side of the corn husk to cover the filling; fold in the other side to cover the first. Fold the pointed tip down to the edge of the filled portion of the husk closest to you to create a packet about 4 inches long and about 1½ inches wide. If the meat filling is visible at the top of the tamale, seal it over with a small daub of masa dough. Set the tamale masa-end up in a vegetable steamer with feet or a colander with a base. Repeat with the remaining corn husks, masa dough, and meat filling, packing the tamales tightly together.

Add enough water to a large pot to come up to but not go above the legs of the steamer or base of the colander that holds the tamales. Set the pot over medium heat and bring the water to a boil. Lower the steamer or colander into the pot and cover the pot. Adjust the heat so that the water maintains a brisk, even simmer. Steam the tamales for 2 hours, adding boiling water as needed to prevent the pot from boiling dry. Let the tamales stand, off the heat, for 10 minutes before serving. *The tamales can be prepared up to 3 days ahead and refrigerated, or up to 1 month ahead and frozen. Rewarm them in a microwave oven, or in a steamer similar to that in which they were cooked.*

makes about 30

tamale pie for company

Southwestern purists frown on tamale pie, but we've always loved its ease of preparation and crowd-pleasing combination of zesty flavors and moist, gooey texture. As long as you think of it as a casual and convenient casserole, and not as a replacement for genuine tamales, it makes great eating. Our everyday version uses homemade—or even canned—chili con carne, but for company we make a rich and rather exotic raisin- and olive-studded shredded pork filling instead. If you're lucky enough to have a tamale factory nearby (we are), you can use purchased tamale dough for the crust; if not, try our green onion variation below.

FILLING
2 tablespoons olive oil
2 to 3 fresh jalapeño chiles,
    stemmed and chopped
2 garlic cloves, peeled and minced
1 teaspoon ground cumin
1 teaspoon dried oregano, crumbled
2½ cups Pork Deshebrada
    (page 130)
1½ cups braising liquid from the
    Pork Deshebrada

½ cup raisins
1 cup corn kernels, canned or de-
    frosted frozen, well drained
½ cup sliced pimiento-stuffed green
    olives
Salt to taste
Freshly ground black pepper to
    taste

DOUGH
2½ cups masa harina de maiz
    (page 253)
½ cup lard, at room temperature
1½ teaspoons baking powder
¾ teaspoon salt
1½ cups chicken broth, homemade
    or canned
5 green onions, trimmed and sliced
    (about ¾ cup)

3 cups (about 12 ounces) Monterey
    Jack cheese or medium-sharp
    cheddar cheese or a combination
    of both
3 cups shredded romaine
2 cups sour cream, whisked until
    smooth and shiny

FOR THE FILLING

In a medium skillet over low heat, warm the olive oil. Add the jalapeños, garlic, cumin, and oregano and cook, covered, stirring once or twice, for 5 minutes. Add the pork deshebrada, braising liquid, and raisins. Raise the heat and simmer briskly, stirring once or twice, for 10 minutes or until the mixture is thick and the liquid has almost entirely evaporated. Stir in the corn, olives, and salt and freshly ground black pepper to taste—the mixture should be very flavorful. *The filling can be prepared up to 1 day ahead. Cool it completely and refrigerate, covered. Return it to room temperature before proceeding with the recipe.*

FOR THE DOUGH

In a food processor, combine the masa harina de maiz, lard, baking powder, and salt and process briefly to blend. With the motor running, add the chicken broth through the feed tube and process until a soft dough is formed. Transfer to a bowl and stir in the green onions. *The dough can be prepared several hours in advance. Cover it tightly and reserve at room temperature.*

TO ASSEMBLE

Position a rack in the middle of the oven and preheat the oven to 350°F.

Transfer half the dough to a deep 3-quart baking dish and, with the back of a spoon, smooth the dough over the bottom and up the sides of the dish to form a crust about ½-inch thick. Spoon the filling into the crust and spread it evenly. Spread the remaining dough evenly over the filling to the sides of the dish. Run the back of the spoon around the sides of the top crust to seal. Sprinkle the pie with the cheese. *The tamale pie can be assembled 1 hour ahead and held, covered, at room temperature.*

Bake about 40 minutes, or until the filling is bubbling, the cheese has melted, and the crust is puffed and lightly set. Let the tamale pie stand on a rack 5 minutes before serving. Accompany it with shredded romaine and sour cream.

For *Chicken Tamale Pie*, substitute an equal amount of Pollo Deshebrada (page 147) for the Pork Deshebrada. Replace the pork braising liquid with 1 cup chicken braising liquid mixed with ½ cup of commercial or homemade red chile purée. Assemble and bake the casserole as directed above.

For *Everyday Tamale Pie*, replace the braising liquid in the dough with canned beef broth and replace pork filling recipe with 4 to 4½ cups canned or homemade chili con carne with beans (such as Norma's Original Recipe Quick 'n' Easy Chili, page 63, or Park's Texas Democrat Chili, page 64). Assemble and bake the casserole as directed above.

serves 6 to 8

super bowl sunday buffet party

Park's Easy Frozen Margaritas (page 239)
Iced Longneck Lonestar Beers

Texas Trash (page 17)
Pico de Gallo (page 3) and Chipotle Salsa del Norte (page 4) and Rancho Bean Dip
(page 15) and Guacamole (page 10) with Tostaditas (page 32) and Chicharrones

Tamale Pie for Company (page 52)
Edythe May's Mango Salad (page 198)
Texas Toast (page 189)

Cowboy Cookies (page 218)
Border Brownies (page 217)
Pineapple-Apricot Empanaditas (page 224)

chili frito pie

This easy, end-of-the-day casserole was created by Daisy Doolin, whose son Elmer Doolin parlayed the purchase of a tostadita-inspired snack chip formula into what is now the conglomerate known as Frito-Lay. The general notion of layering and then baking chili con carne, cheese, onion, and corn chips is so flexible and so personal that a strict recipe is almost unnecessary, but here, to get you started, is a basic formula. Homemade chili makes better chili pie, of course, and for proper texture the Fritos should be regular, not "dip-sized."

6 cups regular-size Fritos corn chips

4 cups (about 1 pound) grated cheese, preferably a combination of Monterey Jack cheese and cheddar cheese

8 cups chili con carne with beans, preferably homemade

1 cup finely chopped onion

6 to 8 pickled jalapeño chiles, stemmed and cut into thin rounds

Fresh or bottled salsa, chopped tomatoes, sour cream, and shredded romaine (optional)

Position a rack in the upper third of the oven and preheat the oven to 350°F.

In a 9- by 13-inch baking dish, spread 4 cups of the Fritos. Scatter half the cheese over the Fritos. Spoon the chili over the cheese. Sprinkle the onions and the pickled jalapeños over the chili. Scatter the remaining Fritos over the casserole. Sprinkle the remaining cheese over the Fritos. Bake 20 to 25 minutes, or until the cheese is melted, the chili is bubbling, and the top is lightly browned. Let the casserole stand 5 minutes on a rack before serving, accompanied, if desired, by salsa, chopped tomatoes, sour cream, and shredded romaine.

serves 8

sopa de pollo
(chicken and corn tortilla casserole)

This "Mexican lasagna" is to enchiladas what tamale pie is to tamales, which is to say it's not quite authentic, but so what? Assembled in easy, do-ahead steps, it's a rich, moist, tasty dish that everyone likes, and never deviating from authenticity at the expense of good eating is not one of our goals. One batch of chicken sopa will feed a modest group, but we often double the recipe and serve the sopa on a buffet table. As part of a festive, multidish spread, two batches will please up to thirty hungry folks.

6 long green chiles
3 tablespoons olive oil
3 cups finely chopped onion
3 garlic cloves, peeled and minced
2 teaspoons ground cumin
1½ teaspoons oregano, crumbled
2 cups chicken broth, homemade or canned
2 cups tomato-based bottled hot salsa
2 teaspoons salt
2 recipes (about 8 cups) Pollo Deshebrada (page 147), chopped

About 2 cups corn oil
24 6-inch corn tortillas
4 cups (about 1 pound) grated cheese, preferably a combination of Monterey Jack cheese and medium-sharp cheddar cheese
16 ounces sour cream, whisked until smooth
Shredded romaine and additional salsa (optional)

In the open flame of a gas burner or under a preheated broiler, roast the long green chiles, turning them, until they are lightly but evenly charred. Steam the chiles in a paper bag, or in a bowl, covered with a plate, until cool. Rub away the burned peel. Stem and seed the chiles and coarsely chop them. There should be about 1 cup.

In a 3-quart nonreactive saucepan over low heat, warm the olive oil. Add the onions, garlic, cumin, and oregano and cook, covered, stirring once or twice, for 15 minutes.

Stir in the chicken broth, salsa, green chiles, and salt and raise the heat. Bring the mixture to a boil, lower the heat slightly, and cook briskly, uncovered, stirring once or twice, for 20 minutes. Cool the sauce to room temperature. Reserve 2 cups of the sauce and combine the remainder with the chicken. *The recipe can be prepared to this point 1 day ahead. Cover and refrigerate the reserved sauce and the chicken mixture separately. Return both to room temperature before proceeding with the recipe.*

Position a rack in the middle of the oven and preheat the oven to 350°F. In a deep skillet, warm about 1 inch of corn oil over medium heat. Using tongs, immerse the tortillas one at a time in the oil, turn them, and then transfer them to absorbent paper. The tortillas should be in the oil no more than a few seconds, and the oil should be hot enough to soften the tortillas but not so hot that the edges begin to crisp.

Arrange 8 of the tortillas in an overlapping layer in the bottom of a 10- by 14-inch baking dish about 2 inches deep. Spread half the chicken over the tortillas. Arrange 8 more of the tortillas in an overlapping layer over the chicken. Sprinkle half the cheese over these tortillas. Spread the remaining chicken mixture over the cheese. Arrange the remaining 8 tortillas over the chicken. Spread the reserved sauce over these tortillas. Sprinkle the remaining cheese over the sauce. Spread the sour cream evenly over the cheese.

Bake about 45 minutes, or until the sopa is crisp around the edges and bubbling and the topping is set. Let the sopa stand on a rack for 5 minutes before serving. Cut it into rectangles to serve, and accompany it with shredded romaine and salsa, if desired.

serves 8 to 10

chicken and bean burrito

Do burritos need defining, or after tacos, aren't these the most familiar of the Southwest's snack foods? Basically, a burrito is a filling rolled into a soft flour tortilla. For us, well-fried beans are always present, along with other interesting (somewhat improvisational) possibilities. Chicken is one modern addition, and a good one, and Michael's Chili con Carne Verde (page 65), which is a classic filling, can't be beat either. In El Paso you may also find a burrito filled with an entire chile relleno (page 193)—odd but good—and breakfast burritos (Burrito Desayuno, page 168) are strong favorites too. Here is a basic plan, from which you are encouraged to branch out; and though this is a recipe for a single burrito, it's a rare meal when two per person isn't more like it.

1 8-inch flour tortilla, at room temperature

⅓ cup Frijoles Refritos (page 179) or canned refried beans

1½ ounces Pollo Deshebrada (page 147)

¼ cup (about 1 ounce) grated Monterey Jack cheese or mozzarella cheese or a combination of both

1 pickled jalapeño chile, stemmed and sliced into thin rounds

½ cup shredded romaine, for garnish

Pico de Gallo (page 3) or any good-quality tomato-based bottled hot salsa

Sour cream, whisked until smooth

Position a rack in the middle of the oven and preheat the oven to 400°F.

Spread the Frijoles Refritos in the center of the tortilla, leaving a 2- to 3-inch border all around. Lay the pollo deshebrada on top of the beans. Sprinkle the cheese over the chicken and lay the jalapeño rounds over the cheese. Fold each side of the tortilla in toward the center. Beginning at the bottom, roll the tortilla up, entirely enclosing the filling and creating a (more or less) leakproof packet. Wrap the burrito tightly in foil. Heat it about 20 minutes, or until the cheese is melted and the filling is steaming hot. Remove the burrito from the foil wrapper and serve it immediately, garnished with shredded romaine and accompanied by salsa and sour cream, if desired.

makes 1 burrito

a homey dinner party for close amigos

Fall Creek Vineyards Texas Sauvignon Blanc Llano County

Grilled Shrimp Quesadillas (page 19) with Chipotle Salsa del Norte (page 4)
Chile con Queso (page 12) with Tostaditas (page 32)

Fall Creek Vineyards Texas Cabernet Sauvignon
Pheasant and Vegetable Potpie (page 142)

Tomatoes and Romaine Lettuce with Avocado-Buttermilk Salad Dressing (page 203)

Vanilla Ice Cream with Kahlúa Chocolate Sauce (page 231)
Sospiras (page 223)

chapter three

chili!
theme and variations on the
state dish

The expression "Them's fightin' words!" seems to have been coined during a discussion between two Texas cooks as to what constitutes a respectable Bowl of Red (redundantly, but accurately, chili con carne—chili with meat—to the uninitiated). 🌶 What could and should be a friendly exploration of a mutual passion often becomes rancorous, with details such as the size of the grind of the meat used in the chili turning otherwise calm folks into raving lunatics (any element of theater in this disagreement can be construed to be strictly intentional). 🌶 As the manufacturers of an excellent chili-seasoning blend we should be in the thick of the fray, but as west Texans we take it all with a grain of garlic salt. 🌶 Around these parts the influences of Old Mexico, New Mexico, and the Pueblo Indians are as strongly felt as anything coming our way from Dallas, Austin, San

Antonio, or Houston, and chili has come to mean a number of different delicious, spicy dishes that a central Texan would probably disdain, leaving, we note with considerable pleasure, all that much more of the fiery stuff for *us* to enjoy.

norma's original recipe quick 'n' easy chili

For years Park and his sister Monica thought Norma had invented chili, her version was so good, and indeed it was this simple, classic (and quick!) recipe that inspired the company's first product—the same chili-powder-seasoning blend we still sell today. Norma has refined her chili over the years and invested it with a full-bodied depth of flavor as well as a mild temperature that makes it particularly suitable for young palates. Because the cooking time is so short, if you do use the coarsely ground chili beef that many Texans prefer, be certain it is from excellent, relatively tender meat (sirloin or filet) and that the meat is scrupulously trimmed before it is ground.

2 tablespoons olive oil
2 cups finely chopped onion
2 pounds ground meat, preferably coarsely ground sirloin
¾ cup (about 3¼ ounces) mild chili powder blend
2 28-ounce cans Italian plum tomatoes, well crushed, with their juices

1 cup beef broth, homemade or canned
4 cans (about 1 pound each) pinto or kidney beans, well drained
1 tablespoon packed light brown sugar
1 tablespoon cider vinegar or red wine vinegar
Salt

In a 5-quart nonreactive Dutch oven or flameproof casserole over low heat, warm the olive oil. Add the onions and cook, covered, stirring once or twice, for 15 minutes. Add the meat and cook, stirring occasionally, for about 15 minutes, or until it is no longer pink. Add the chili powder blend and cook, stirring once or twice, for 5 minutes. Stir in the tomatoes and beef broth, raise the heat, and bring the chili to a boil. Lower the heat, partially cover, and cook, stirring often, for 30 minutes. The chili will be very thick.

Stir in the beans, brown sugar, and vinegar. Adjust the seasoning, adding salt to taste. Cook another 5 minutes, or until heated through and steaming. *The chili can be prepared up to 3 days in advance. Cool it completely and refrigerate it, covered. Rewarm it over low heat, thinning it with water if necessary and stirring often.*

makes 3½ quarts, serving 10

park's texas democrat chili

Park's medium-hot chili, with roasted red peppers, cactus pads, and red wine, is for the culinarily (if not the politically) liberal. Serve it at your next fund-raiser—it's a winner! This can also be made using domestically raised venison or buffalo meat.

3 large heavy sweet peppers, red, orange, or yellow or a combination

5 strips bacon, preferably mesquite-smoked, chopped

1 tablespoon olive oil

2 cups coarsely chopped onion

2 garlic cloves, peeled and minced

2 fresh jalapeño chiles, stemmed and minced

2 pounds beef stewing meat (such as chuck), in well-trimmed ½-inch cubes

½ cup mild chili powder blend

4 cups beef broth, homemade or canned

1 cup dry red wine

1 cup canned crushed tomatoes with added purée

2 16-ounce cans pinto or kidney beans or a combination of both, drained and rinsed

1 14-ounce jar nopalitos, rinsed, drained, and chopped

In the open flame of a gas burner, or under a preheated electric broiler, roast the sweet peppers, turning them, until the peels are evenly charred. In a bowl covered with a plate or in a closed paper bag, steam the peppers until they are cool. Rub away the burned peel, stem and core the peppers, and coarsely chop the flesh.

In a heavy 5-quart nonreactive pot over low heat, combine the bacon and olive oil. Cook, stirring once or twice, until the bacon is crisp, 10 to 12 minutes. With a slotted spoon, transfer the bacon to absorbent paper to drain.

Add the onions, garlic, and jalapeños to the oil in the pot and cook over low heat, stirring once or twice, for 10 minutes. Add the beef and cook, stirring often, until it is no longer pink, about 10 minutes. Stir in the chili powder blend and cook 5 minutes. Stir in the beef broth, red wine, and crushed tomatoes. Raise the heat and bring the chili to a boil. Partially cover, lower the heat, and simmer, stirring occasionally, for 1½ hours. Uncover the chili and cook, stirring often, until the meat is very tender, 30 to 40 minutes. Stir in the roasted sweet peppers, beans, nopalitos, and bacon and cook another 5 minutes, or until heated through and steaming. Adjust the seasoning. *The chili can be prepared at least a day ahead. Cool it to room temperature and refrigerate it. Warm it up slowly over low heat before serving.*

makes 2½ quarts, serving 8

michael's chili con carne verde

Michael was the founding chef of The Manhattan Chili Co., in Greenwich Village, and his chili verde with pork draws its inspiration from New Mexican and Pueblo Indian dishes. His recipe is unconventional in technique but nevertheless results in an authentically thick and fiery stew containing little more than tender, shredded pork and poblano chiles. Enjoy a bowlful, accompanied by plenty of warmed flour tortillas, or enclose it, along with refried beans, in a green chile burrito (page 168). You may substitute long green chiles for the poblanos; if you do, increase the jalapeños. Traditional chili verde, as a rule, is absolutely incendiary.

12 large poblano chiles
1 6- to 7-pound pork shoulder roast (*calas*), with bone
¼ cup rendered bacon fat or olive oil
6 cups chicken broth, homemade or canned
6 cups chopped onion

8 garlic cloves, peeled and minced
4 fresh jalapeño chiles, stemmed and minced
1 tablespoon dried oregano, crumbled
¼ cup unbleached all-purpose flour
About 1½ teaspoons salt

In the open flame of a gas burner, or under a preheated electric broiler, roast the poblanos, turning them, until the peels are evenly charred. In a bowl covered with a plate or in a closed paper bag, steam the poblanos until they are cool. Rub away the burned peel, stem and core the peppers, and cut the flesh into ¼-inch-wide strips.

Position a rack in the middle of the oven and preheat the oven to 325°F.

If the roast has a thick layer of external fat on one side, cut away as much of it as is possible. In a heavy 5-quart Dutch oven or flameproof casserole, warm the bacon fat over medium-high heat. Pat the pork shoulder dry, add it to the fat, and cook, turning occasionally, until it is well browned on all sides, about 20 minutes. Add the chicken broth, onions, and garlic, cover and bake, turning the roast once at the approximate halfway point, until it is very tender, about 4 hours.

Cool the roast to room temperature in the braising liquid, then transfer it to a plate, wrap it well, and refrigerate overnight. Pour the braising liquid through a strainer into a bowl, pressing hard with the back of a spoon to extract all the juices. Discard the solids. Cover the liquid and refrigerate overnight.

The following day trim any fat from the roast and shred the meat (fingers work best). Scrape the chilled fat from the surface of the braising liquid and reserve ¼ cup of it, discarding the rest of it. Add enough water to the braising liquid to equal 7 cups.

In a 5-quart pot over medium heat, melt the reserved fat. Add the jalapeños and oregano, lower the heat, and cook for 5 minutes, stirring often. Stir in the flour and cook, stirring constantly, for 3 minutes; do not brown. Whisk in the braising liquid. Stir the shredded pork and the rajas into the liquid. Bring to a boil, lower the heat, and simmer, partially covered, stirring occasionally, for 2 hours. Add salt to taste, adjust the seasoning, and simmer another 20 to 30 minutes. The chili should be very thick, the pork very tender, and the chiles virtually dissolved into the stew.

makes 3½ quarts, serving 10

school night chili supper

Ice-cold Milk

Classic Nachos (page 26)

Norma's Original Recipe Quick 'n' Easy Chili (page 63)
Garnishes of Grated Cheese, Sour Cream, and Chopped Onions
White Rice
Good Old Corn Bread (page 191)

Whipped Mexican Chocolate (page 242)
Bizcochos (page 220)

red kidney bean chili with avocados
and onion relish

Here is a meatless chili for these modern (low-cholesterol) times. If this sounds like a cruel penance to you, consider that this chili is altogether spicy, rich, and very substantial. The only thing missing is the meat, and thanks to the chewy, satisfying texture of the kidney beans, you won't miss it. The chocolate adds a silky texture and its slight bitterness balances the sweetness of the tomatoes. The usual chili toppings of cheese and sour cream are tasty here, but for a change of pace, consider our crunchy, salsalike marinated red onion relish plus wedges of avocado.

CHILI

1 pound dried red kidney beans, picked over and rinsed
¼ cup olive oil
3 cups chopped onion
2 fresh jalapeño chiles, stemmed and minced
4 garlic cloves, peeled and minced
2 tablespoons mild chili powder blend
1½ tablespoons ground cumin
1 tablespoon dried oregano, crumbled
1 35-ounce can Italian-style plum tomatoes, crushed, with their juices
5 cups chicken broth, homemade or canned
2 large heavy sweet peppers (red, yellow, or orange), stemmed, cored, and coarsely diced
5 teaspoons salt
1 10-ounce package frozen corn kernels, thawed and drained
1 ounce (1 square) unsweetened chocolate, grated

RELISH

2 cups diced red onion
3 tablespoons white wine vinegar
2 tablespoons olive oil
⅛ teaspoon sugar
⅛ teaspoon salt
½ cup minced cilantro
2 buttery-ripe black-skinned avocados, pitted and cut into thin unpeeled wedges, for garnish

continued

In a large bowl, combine the beans with water to cover by at least 3 inches and let them soak for 24 hours. Drain.

In a 5-quart nonreactive pan over medium heat, warm the olive oil. Add the onions, jalapeños, garlic, chili powder blend, cumin, and oregano and lower the heat. Cook, covered, stirring once or twice, for 15 minutes. Add the tomatoes and their juices, the chicken broth and drained beans. Raise the heat and bring to a boil. Cover, lower the heat slightly, and cook, stirring occasionally, for 50 minutes. Stir in the sweet peppers and salt and cook, covered, stirring often, for another 30 minutes, or until the beans are tender. Stir in the corn. Remove from the heat and stir in the chocolate. Adjust the seasoning. *The chili can be prepared to this point up to 2 days ahead. Cool it to room temperature and refrigerate, covered.*

In a medium bowl, combine the red onions, vinegar, olive oil, sugar, and salt and let stand 30 minutes. Stir in the cilantro.

Rewarm the chili over low heat, stirring often, until steaming. Ladle the chili into bowls and garnish each serving with a generous spoonful of the onion relish and several avocado wedges.

serves 8

corona ranch chili con carne colorado

Named for an old Kerr family property located in central New Mexico, this is perhaps the purest and simplest form "chili" can take. Little more than a savory, medium-hot stew of cubed pork and puréed red chile pods, it usually shows up on restaurant menus (especially New Mexico–style menus) along with a fiery green chile by way of contrast. Eat it from a bowl with warm flour tortillas or use it as the main ingredient in a batch of Tostadas Compuestas (page 47). Order the cubed meat from the butcher, or if you're good with a boning knife, trim it out yourself from a 5-pound pork shoulder roast (*calas*). Though it's not traditional, you can stretch the finished chili by adding a 1-pound can of well-drained black beans. The recipe will then serve six as a main course.

¼ pound (about 12 large) dry red
    chile pods
2 or 3 chiles de arbol
1½ cups water
3 tablespoons olive oil
2 cups finely chopped onion
4 garlic cloves, peeled and minced

2½ pounds pork shoulder meat, in
    well-trimmed ¾-inch cubes
1 teaspoon ground cumin
1 teaspoon dried oregano, crumbled
1½ teaspoons salt
5 cups beef broth or chicken broth,
    homemade or canned

Stem the red chile pods and the chiles de arbol. Slit them open (kitchen scissors work well here). Shake out as many of the seeds as possible and rinse the chiles briefly under cold running water. Tear or snip them into 1-inch pieces.

Bring the water to a boil and pour it over the chile pieces in a medium heat-proof bowl. Cover the bowl with a pot lid or a plate and let the chile pieces stand, stirring them once or twice, until the water is cool.

With a slotted spoon, transfer the softened chile pieces to the jar of a blender or the work bowl of a food processor. Process briefly, scraping down the sides of the jar. Add some of the soaking water and process again. Continue adding water, blending, and then scraping down the sides until the water has all been used and the chile purée is smooth. Transfer the purée to a strainer set over a bowl. Add 2 tablespoons hot tap water to the blender and purée briefly to rinse the blades and the inside. Add this residue to the purée in the strainer. Force the puréed chiles through the strainer with a stiff rubber spatula, discarding any seeds and tough bits of peel remaining in the strainer. There should be about 1¼ cups purée. If there is more, use it all. If there is less, soak, simmer, and purée additional chiles. *The purée can be stored, well-covered, in the refrigerator for up to 3 days, or frozen for up to 1 month.*

In a Dutch oven or heavy flameproof casserole over low heat, warm the olive oil. Add the onions and garlic and cook, covered, stirring once or twice, for 10 minutes. Add the cubed pork, chile purée, cumin, oregano, and salt and cook, tossing and stirring often, for 5 minutes. Stir in the broth, raise the heat, and bring to a boil. Lower the heat, partially cover the pan, and cook, stirring occasionally, until the meat is very tender and the dish has thickened, about 2 hours. Adjust the seasoning. *The chili can be prepared up to 3 days ahead. Cool it completely and refrigerate it, covered. Warm it over low heat, stirring often, before serving.*

serves 4 or 6

chili buffet for a crowd

Assorted Cold Texas and Mexican Beers

Guacamole (page 10) and Pico de Gallo (page 3) and Santos's Salsa Verde (page 6)
with Tostaditas (page 32) and Chicharrones

Park's Texas Democrat Chili (page 64)
Norma's Original Recipe Quick 'n' Easy Chili (page 63)
Corona Ranch Chili con Carne Colorado (page 69)
Garnishes of Grated Cheese, Sour Cream, Chopped Onions, and Pickled Jalapeños
Double Corn Spoon Bread with Chiles and Cheese (page 190)

"Aunt Hazel Millican's" Sweet Chocolate Cake (page 208)
Peach Cobbler (page 210) with Amaretto Whipped Cream

chapter four

playing with fire
barbecue, grilling, and smoking

Rising up into the clear, thin air of the Southwest is the fine, fragrant smoke of a thousand fires. ✿ Mesquite, hickory, pecan, peach, and even piñon woods are lazily ablaze, cooking and preserving meats, seafood, and vegetables. ✿ As essential as the flavors of corn, chiles, cumin, garlic, cilantro, and oregano are in defining the food of the region, so, too, the scent and taste of woodsmoke find their way seductively into more and more of what we cook every day.

sorting it out

Barbecue in Texas originally meant (and sometimes still means) meat that was cooked sealed into a coal-filled pit in the earth. ✿ This vast effort requires expertise and time and there are still a few wizened pit masters who will show up with a back hoe and large sections of beef or pork carcasses and spend twenty-four hours feeding you and a few hundred of your friends sublime food. (Nowadays, though, this is such an extravagant event it's usually reserved for visiting Japanese industrialists or the President.) Commercial barbecue places are a combination workshop/restaurant, where smaller, permanent smoking chambers (of cinder block, etc.) slow-cook brisket, ribs, hot sausage links, and pork roasts to succulent tenderness and you can just walk in and order a plateful. There are now home smokers, ranging from the Hondo, a four-wheel, cast-iron firebox the size of a Volkswagen to such affordable electric water smokers as those from Brinkman and Rival. Such slow, moist, and smoky cooking methods approximate, with varying degrees of success, the pit barbecue taste and texture. Grilling is a quick cooking method over hot coals, and due to the presence of barbecue sauce, is what the rest of America calls barbecue when they think of hamburgers, hot dogs, and ribs, as well as seafood, vegetables, breads, and many other things.

El Pasoans appreciate the subtle but important distinctions between these cooking methods and celebrate them equally. In this chapter we have tried to sample everything from old-fashioned, slow-cooked brisket and familiar grilled burgers to such con-

temporary fare as hickory-smoked turkey breast and grilled tuna steaks. Whether

quick and hot or slow and easy, fire and smoke add their pungent flavor and aroma to all

of the following Kerr family favorites.

home smoker barbecue brisket of beef

One of the great triumphs of Texas cooking is barbecued brisket of beef. A visit to one of the rudimentary establishments specializing in brisket, usually located on a busy main artery and usually crowded (if the barbecue is good) with satisfied diners, is an essential Texas experience. While the minimal ambience, hickory-smoke-laden air, ritual ohing and ahing, and utterly cheap paper plates and flimsy paper napkins are all part of enjoying the experience, the brisket itself can be successfully duplicated at home, following this easy recipe and using one of the several simple and inexpensive water smokers on the market.

4 chunks of mesquite or hickory
  smoking wood
1 5-pound first-cut brisket of beef
¼ cup unsulfured molasses

1 tablespoon freshly ground black
  pepper
1 tablespoon sweet paprika
1½ teaspoons salt

Soak the wood chunks in water for 2 hours. Set up an electric water smoker outdoors in a place shielded from the wind.

Brush the brisket evenly on both sides with the molasses. In a small bowl, stir together the freshly ground black pepper, paprika, and salt. Sprinkle this mixture evenly over the brisket and pat it into the molasses.

Drain the wood chunks. Place them in the smoker and set the basin of water in place according to the smoker manufacturer's directions. Set the brisket fat-side up on the lower rack of the smoker and put the lid in place. Smoke the brisket, adding additional water to the basin in the smoker if necessary, until it is very tender, 4½ to 5½ hours, depending on the wind, weather, and smoker you use.

Let the brisket rest on a cutting board, tented with foil, for 10 minutes, before slicing it very thinly across the grain and at a slight angle.

serves 8 to 10

smoke signals barbecue sauce

To be honest, we rarely make barbecue sauce at home. As the manufacturers of what we consider two very fine sauces, we are likelier to crack open a jar of one or the other instead. Still, one mark of a true pit master is a quintessential sauce, available on the table for slathering or drizzling (usually onto succulent smoked brisket) as the diner prefers. Composed of multiple secret ingredients, such a sauce often includes, in the Frankenstein spirit, a host of unlikely elements brought into some kind of harmony by the will of its creator. Here is our contribution to the genre—a sauce including smoky chipotles along with a touch of hickory smoke flavor—one that is equally at home on grilled chicken, shrimp, burgers, brisket, and ribs.

3 tablespoons olive oil
1 cup minced onion
3 garlic cloves, peeled and minced
1 tablespoon mild chili powder blend
1 28-ounce can crushed tomatoes with added purée
1 12-ounce bottle amber beer, such as Dos Equis
1 cup tomato-based bottled hot salsa
½ cup catsup
¼ cup packed light brown sugar
4 chipotles adobado, minced
3 tablespoons adobo from the chipotle can
2 tablespoons cider vinegar
2 tablespoons unsulfured molasses
½ teaspoon liquid hickory smoke flavoring
½ teaspoon salt

In a heavy 3-quart saucepan over low heat, warm the olive oil. Add the onions and garlic and cook, covered, stirring once or twice, for 10 minutes. Stir in the chili powder blend and cook, covered, for 5 minutes.

Stir in the crushed tomatoes, beer, salsa, catsup, brown sugar, chipotles, adobo, vinegar, molasses, liquid smoke, and salt and bring to a simmer. Cook, partially covered, stirring once or twice, until the sauce has thickened slightly and is shiny, about 30 minutes.

Cool the sauce to room temperature and, if you prefer a smooth sauce, force it through the medium blade of a food mill or purée it in a food processor. Transfer it to a storage container and refrigerate. *The sauce will keep for several weeks in the refrigerator or can be transferred to a number of smaller containers and frozen for up to 3 months.*

makes about 2 quarts

✦

a bar-b-cue dinner

Rio Grande Lemonade (page 242) or Lone Star Longneck Beers

Texas Party Brisket (page 118) or Home Smoker Barbecue Brisket of Beef (page 76)
Smoked Spareribs with Tabasco, Honey, and Garlic (page 83)
Smoke Signals Barbecue Sauce (page 77)
Jalapeño-Pineapple Coleslaw (page 199)
Roasted New Potato Salad with Green Chiles (page 201)

"Aunt Hazel Millican's" Sweet Chocolate Cake (page 208)

✦

smoked red chile–rubbed cornish hens

We think of these smoky, slightly *picante* little birds as picnic food because they're so good cold and so much fun to eat by hand. Even after a lengthy smoking Cornish hens stay wonderfully moist and juicy and there's plenty of lip smacking and finger licking when these are featured on a menu. For ease of serving, as well as for a longer, more intense smoking period, we use larger birds and cut them in half with poultry shears after smoking them.

4 chunks of mesquite smoking
   wood
4 large Cornish hens (about 1¾
   pounds each), preferably fresh

4 tablespoons olive oil
8 teaspoons mild chili powder blend

Soak the wood chunks in water for 2 hours. Set up an electric water smoker outdoors in a place shielded from the wind.

Remove the giblets from the Cornish hens and reserve them for another use. Pull out any visible fat from the cavities and with kitchen twine tie the feet of each hen together. Rub each hen evenly with 1 tablespoon of olive oil and then sprinkle it evenly with 2 teaspoons of chili powder blend, rubbing it firmly into the skin.

Drain the wood chunks. Place them in the smoker and set the basin of water in place according to the smoker manufacturer's directions. Set the hens on the lower rack of the smoker, cover it, and smoke them for about 2½ hours, depending on the wind, weather, and smoker you use, or until a thigh when pricked at its thickest yields clear yellow juices.

Cool the Cornish hens on a rack to room temperature. Using poultry shears or a long sharp knife, cut them in half lengthwise. Serve them at room temperature.

serves 8

a portable picnic

A Thermos of Rio Grande Lemonade (page 242)

Corn, Black Bean, and Roasted Red Pepper Salsa (page 7) with Tostaditas (page 32)
Texas Trash (page 17)

Smoked Red Chile–Rubbed Cornish Hens (page 79)
Jalapeño-Pineapple Coleslaw (page 199)
Roasted New Potato Salad with Green Chiles (page 201)

Cowboy Cookies (page 218)
Border Brownies (page 217)
Fresh Fruit

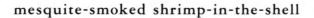

mesquite-smoked shrimp-in-the-shell

Seafood is not plentiful in landlocked El Paso, and when it does get here it's expensive. The one exception is shrimp. Abundantly fished from both the Gulf of Mexico and the Gulf of California, it arrives in our supermarkets in excellent condition, often at breathtakingly low prices. When that happens, we fire up the smoker for a batch of these irresistible crustaceans. Smoking them in the shell makes for messier eating, but there is less shrinkage and, thanks to the fat that is retained, more genuine shrimp flavor. We like them plain (perhaps with a shake of bottled habañero hot sauce) and adore them dipped into Smoked Jalapeño-Lime Mayonnaise (page 23) or Peppery Garlic-Lime Mayonnaise (page 98).

2 chunks of mesquite smoking wood	3 tablespoons fresh lime juice
1½ pounds (about 36) medium shrimp, in their shells	3 tablespoons olive oil

Soak the wood chunks in water for 2 hours. Set up an electric water smoker outdoors in a place shielded from the wind.

Select a disposable foil pan just large enough to hold the shrimp more or less in a single layer while sitting on a smoker rack. In the foil pan toss together the shrimp, lime juice, and olive oil.

Drain the wood chunks. Place them in the smoker and set the basin of water in place according to the smoker manufacturer's directions. Set the pan of shrimp on the lower rack, cover the smoker, and smoke the shrimp, stirring them every 10 minutes, until they are pink, curled, and cooked through, about 40 minutes, depending on the wind, weather, and smoker you use.

Cool the shrimp to room temperature and serve them in the shell.

serves 6, if you're lucky

apple-marinated hickory-smoked turkey breast

This easy smoked turkey breast is a holiday mainstay for both Kerr households, providing plenty of elegant eating on an open-house buffet (one Thanksgiving even replacing the regular roasted bird altogether), and then supplying plenty of leftovers for impromptu nibbling until the bones are bare. Our favorite snack is a sandwich of thin-sliced hickory-smoked turkey, home-smoked chipotles (page 205), and plenty of mayo from a jar, all piled high on a crusty hard roll. Add frosty beer to taste.

3 chunks of hickory smoking wood
4 cups unfiltered apple cider
1 cup chicken broth, homemade or
  canned
1 bone-in fresh turkey breast (about
  5 pounds)

1 head of garlic, separated into
  cloves (no need to peel)
1 small onion, peeled and sliced
12 black peppercorns
6 bay leaves

Soak the wood chunks in water for 2 hours. Set up an electric water smoker outdoors in a place shielded from the wind.

In a large bowl, pour the apple cider and chicken broth over the turkey breast and marinate, turning once or twice, for 1 hour.

Drain the wood chunks and place them in the smoker according to the smoker manufacturer's directions. Pour the cider mixture into the smoker's water basin. Add the garlic cloves, onion slices, peppercorns, and bay leaves. Add additional water to fill the basin and set it in place in the smoker. Set the turkey breast on the lower rack of the smoker and set the lid in place. Smoke the turkey, adding additional water to the basin if necessary, for 3½ to 4½ hours, depending on the wind, weather, and smoker you use, or until an instant-reading thermometer inserted into the thickest part of the breast registers 160°F.

Transfer the turkey to a cutting board, tent it with foil, and let it stand 10 minutes before carving if it is to be served warm, or cool it to room temperature before slicing if it is to be served cold. *The turkey can be smoked several days ahead (though it will not be as moist) and refrigerated, well wrapped. Return it to room temperature before serving.*

serves 8 to 10

smoked spareribs with tabasco, honey, and garlic

The typical west Texas barbecue combination plate includes, along with the requisite brisket, two or three deliciously meaty, fragrantly smoky spareribs. The spareribs in this recipe will feed three or four, or six if they're teamed up with plenty of brisket and other fixin's. Though there is a daunting amount of hot sauce involved, the ribs end up only pleasantly spicy.

3 chunks of mesquite or hickory
    smoking wood
½ cup honey
½ cup Tabasco or other hot pepper
    sauce
8 garlic cloves, peeled and crushed
    through a press

2 teaspoons salt
2 sides regular (not baby back)
    spareribs (about 5 pounds total),
    chine bones cracked for easier
    serving

Soak the wood chunks in water for 2 hours. Set up an electric water smoker outdoors in a place shielded from the wind.

In a small bowl, stir together the honey, Tabasco sauce, garlic, and salt. Pour the mixture over the spareribs in a shallow bowl and turn the ribs several times to coat them well. Cover and let them stand at room temperature, turning occasionally, for 1 hour.

Drain the wood chunks. Place them in the smoker and set the basin of water in place according to the smoker manufacturer's directions. Set the ribs on the lower rack of the smoker, using the specially designed rib holder if you have one, and set the lid in place. Smoke the ribs, adding additional water to the basin in the smoker if necessary, until they are very tender, 4½ to 5½ hours, depending on the wind, weather, and smoker you use.

Let the ribs rest on a cutting board, tented with foil, for 10 minutes. Cut them apart with a sharp knife to serve. *The ribs can be prepared several hours ahead and reheated, wrapped in foil, in a 350°F oven.*

serves 3 to 6

carne asada a la tampiquena
(tampico-style steak combination plate)

Carne asada means roasted meat, and its simplest and commonest form is a grilled steak, topped, perhaps, with rajas of poblano or other green chiles. Far more delicious and baroque is the following, the speciality of a Mexico City restaurateur originally from Tampico. This is one combination plate that even Mexican purists admire. Although it is a relatively recent invention (1940 or so), it is now widely found in restaurants throughout Mexico, and while the components vary slightly from cook to cook, the heart of the matter is always a grilled or pan-fried steak of varying quality, grandly accompanied by enchiladas, beans, guacamole, salsa, rajas, cheese, and so on. Because of the multiple operations involved, it's a dish that is more suited to restaurant preparation, but it can be done at home—it's a lot of fun and people are always impressed. The meat is typically something fairly resilient, butterflied with the grain into very thin sheets, but we have also enjoyed sliced skirt steak and, even on occasion, tenderloin or filet. In the authentic preparation a square of nonmelting cheese (*panela*) is broiled and served beside the steak, but at Martino's in Juárez the cheese (*asadero*) comes melted on top of the meat. Perhaps it's the cheeseburger lover in us, but that is the method we prefer. The tacos we add to the plate are also a Martino's touch, but you can omit them and serve each guest two enchiladas instead.

In any case, if you have a willing volunteer (or two) to supervise the various indoor and outdoor operations and to assist with plating and serving, things will go much more smoothly. In order to avoid requiring a half recipe of the enchiladas, we made this a recipe for twelve, though in truth, if you can divide accurately and don't mind random leftovers, it can be prepared for fewer. Accompany the Carne Asada a la Tampiquena with Pico de Gallo (page 3) and warmed corn tortillas (page 257) or Texas Toast (page 189).

6 poblano chiles
⅔ cup fresh lime juice
⅓ cup olive oil
4 garlic cloves, crushed through a
    press
½ teaspoon salt

½ teaspoon freshly ground black
    pepper
4½ pounds skirt, filet, or other
    steak of your choice, in 12 well-
    trimmed 6-ounce steaks
1½ pounds Monterey Jack cheese,
    sliced

1 recipe Frijoles de Olla (page 178) or 2 recipes Frijoles Refritos (page 179), heated

1 recipe Enchiladas de Pollo Verdes (page 38)

1 recipe Red Pork Street Tacos (page 44)

1 recipe Guacamole (page 10)

Tostaditas (page 32)

In the open flame of a gas burner or under a preheated broiler, roast the poblanos, turning them, until they are lightly but evenly charred. Steam the poblanos in a paper bag, or in a bowl, covered with a plate, until cool. Rub away the burned peel. Stem and seed the poblanos and cut them into ¼-inch-wide strips.

In a shallow nonreactive dish, stir together the lime juice, olive oil, garlic, salt, and freshly ground black pepper. Add the steaks, coat them on both sides, and marinate, covered, at room temperature, turning them once or twice more, for 1 hour.

Preheat a gas grill (medium-high) or light a charcoal fire and let it burn down until the coals are evenly white.

Preheat the broiler.

Position a rack on the grill about 6 inches above the heat source. Lay the steaks on the grill, baste them with half of the marinade, and cover the grill. Cook the steaks, turning them once and basting them with the remaining marinade, until they are medium-rare (about 8 minutes total, depending on the cut of meat you have chosen). Transfer the steaks to a large broiler-proof pan that will hold them comfortably in a single layer.

Divide the rajas evenly over the steaks and divide the cheese evenly over the rajas. Set the pan of steaks under the broiler and cook just until the cheese is melted and lightly browned, 1 to 2 minutes.

Transfer the steaks to heated plates. Spoon beans onto the plates. Set an enchilada on each plate. Place a taco on each plate. Spoon a generous dollop of guacamole onto each plate, stick 3 or 4 tostaditas into each dollop of guacamole and also, if you are using them, into each dollop of Frijoles Refritos. Serve immediately.

serves 12

grilled jalapeño honey mustard chicken

We think our Sweet Texas Fire is the best sweet/hot mustard on the market and use it often in easy, nontraditional marinades like this one. (You may substitute your favorite honey mustard augmented by two or three finely minced pickled jalapeños.) Serve the chicken as knife-and-fork food (perhaps on top of a crisp Caesar salad) or make sandwiches on toasted buns. Park dices any leftover chicken and uses it on quesadillas.

½ cup jalapeño honey mustard
¼ cup orange marmalade
1 tablespoon soy sauce

3 pounds skinless, boneless chicken breasts, halved and trimmed of fat and connective tissue
2 cups fruitwood smoking chips

In a small bowl, stir together the mustard, marmalade, and soy sauce. In a shallow nonreactive dish, combine the marinade and the chicken breasts and let them stand at room temperature, covered, turning them once or twice, for 1 hour.

Soak the fruitwood chips in water for at least 30 minutes.

Preheat a gas grill (medium-high) or light a charcoal fire and let it burn down until the coals are evenly white. Drain the wood chips, scatter them over the grill stones or coals and position a rack about 6 inches above the heat source. Cover the grill.

When the chips are smoking, lay the chicken breasts on the grill rack. Cover and cook them 3 minutes. Turn the breasts, baste them with some of the remaining marinade, cover, and cook 3 more minutes. Turn them again, baste them with the remaining marinade, and grill them another 3 to 5 minutes, or until the chicken is just cooked through without being dry. Remove the breasts from the grill immediately and serve them hot, warm, or cool.

serves 4 to 6

a fajitas parrilla

Park's Easy Frozen Margaritas (page 239)
Iced Mexican Beers

Queso Fundido on the Grill (page 20) with Warmed Corn Tortillas
Rancho Bean Dip (page 15) with Tostaditas (page 32)

Fajitas on the Grill (page 92) with Pico de Gallo (page 3) and
Mantequilla de los Pobres (page 11)
Grilled Corn on the Cob with Lime Butter and Chili Powder (page 183)

Mango-Peach Ice Cream with Dulce Crunch (page 230)
Border Brownies (page 217)

---

grilled tuna with orange-chili marinade

The simple marinade on these tuna steaks gives a sharp edge of flavor and a touch of color that make for very good eating, especially when accompanied by a generous dollop of Corn, Black Bean, and Roasted Red Pepper Salsa (page 7) or of Tropical Mango Salsa (page 8). This recipe also works for shark or swordfish steaks, and on the East Coast bluefish filets.

½ cup fresh orange juice
½ cup packed cilantro (stems may be included)
⅓ cup red chile paste, homemade or commercial
¼ cup olive oil
2 garlic cloves, peeled and chopped

1 chipotle adobado, with clinging sauce
4 1-inch-thick tuna steaks (2½ to 3 pounds total)
2 cups mesquite wood grilling chips
Salt to taste

In a blender or a small food processor, combine the orange juice, cilantro, chile paste, olive oil, garlic cloves, and chipotle with its adobado. Blend until smooth. In a shallow nonreactive dish, combine the marinade and the tuna steaks and let them stand at room temperature, covered, turning them once or twice, for 1 hour.

Soak the wood chips in water for at least 30 minutes.

Preheat a gas grill (medium-high) or light a charcoal fire and let it burn down until the coals are evenly white. Drain the wood chips, scatter them over the grill stones or the coals and position a rack about 6 inches above the heat source. Cover the grill. When the chips are smoking, lay the tuna steaks on the grill. Baste them with any remaining marinade, cover the grill, and cook 4 minutes. Turn the tuna steaks and cook them another 3 to 4 minutes or until they are lightly browned but still pink at the center. Remove them from the heat, season them with salt to taste, and serve immediately.

serves 4

a dove dinner

Kay Queveda's Chile con Queso with Crab (page 13)
Tostaditas (page 32)

Smothered Doves (page 140)
White Rice
Calabacitas con Crema (page 185)
Calico Corn (page 182)
Warm Flour Tortillas

Peach Cobbler (page 210)

el paso chile cheeseburgers

A touch of sour cream, green chiles, and green onions, plus a grilling over smoky wood chips, gives these cheeseburgers real flavor and character. We like them with Smoked Jalapeño-Lime Mayonnaise, but catsup and mustard work fine too.

3 long green chiles
2 cups mesquite or hickory wood
   smoking chips
2 pounds ground chuck, not too
   lean
2 green onions, trimmed and thinly
   sliced (about ⅓ cup)
3 tablespoons sour cream
½ teaspoon salt
½ teaspoon freshly ground black
   pepper

6 ounces Monterey Jack cheese with
   jalapeños, sliced
6 hamburger buns, split
2 medium tomatoes, sliced
6 leaves of romaine or other crisp
   lettuce
Smoked Jalapeño-Lime Mayonnaise
   (page 23)

In the open flame of a gas burner or under a preheated broiler, roast the long green chiles, turning them, until they are lightly but evenly charred. Steam the chiles in a paper bag, or in a bowl, covered with a plate, until cool. Rub away the burned peel. Stem and seed the chiles and coarsely chop them. There should be about ⅓ cup.

Soak the wood chips in water for at least 30 minutes.

In a medium bowl, stir together the ground chuck, green chiles, green onions, sour cream, salt, and freshly ground black pepper. Lightly form the meat into 6 equal patties about 1-inch thick.

Preheat a gas grill (medium-high) or light a charcoal fire and let it burn down until the coals are evenly white. Drain the wood chips and scatter them over the grill stones or coals. Position the grill rack about 6 inches above the heat source and lower the cover. When the chips are smoking, lay the hamburger patties on the grill and cook them, covered, for 4 minutes. Turn the patties, top them with the cheese and cook them, covered, another 3 to 4 minutes (for medium-rare), or until the cheese is melted. During the last 2 to 3 minutes of the grilling time you may want to toast the hamburger buns, cut-sides-down, on the grill.

Assemble the cheeseburgers on the buns and serve, passing the sliced tomatoes, romaine, and smoked jalapeño-lime mayonnaise separately.

serves 6

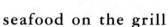

seafood on the grill

Fall Creek Texas Llano County Sauvignon Blanc

Grilled Shrimp (page 22) with Peppery Garlic-Lime Mayonnaise (page 98)

Grilled Tuna with Orange-Chili Marinade (page 88)
Tropical Mango Salsa (page 8)
Ensalada de Nopalitos (page 202)
Texas Three-Bean Salad (page 200)
Flour Tortillas Warmed on the Grill

Forti's Almond Flan (page 234)

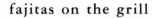

fajitas on the grill

With so much clear, dry weather (more sunny days than almost any other city in the United States), El Pasoans who grill outdoors do so nearly year-round. Except during one or two very cold months (when we make Winter Fajitas, page 114), some kind of fajita or other gets grilled up by the Kerrs almost every week. This dish, by the way, rarely shows up on El Paso restaurant menus—it's more a central Texas speciality, but we love it anyway. The appeal, we think, is in the improvisational, assemble-your-own spirit of the dish: Tucking a little of this and a little of that into warmed tortillas is a very attractive and informal way to eat. Here is a grand mixed fajita *parrilla* ("grill")—skirt steak, lobster, chicken, *and* shrimp—a real party. On simpler occasions we halve the marinade and use just one or two of the main components.

Two practical notes: The live lobsters can be replaced with 4 defrosted frozen lobster tails, slightly undercooked according to the directions on the package. And, although some grill manufacturers warn against heavy basting, Park has always just dumped all the remaining marinade over the fajitas on the grill (the fuming cloud of steam and smoke is full of flavor) and he reports it has not harmed his grill.

2 tablespoons plus 1 teaspoon salt
2 live lobsters (about 1½ pounds each)
2 cups tomato-based bottled hot salsa
1 cup chopped red onion
1 cup packed fresh cilantro (stems may be used)
4 fresh jalapeño chiles, stemmed and chopped
¼ cup gold tequila
¼ cup fresh lime juice
1 cup amber beer, such as Dos Equis

2¼ pounds (2 or 3 pieces) skirt steak
1½ pounds boneless, skinless chicken breasts, halved and trimmed of fat and connective tissue
1 pound (about 18) large shrimp, shelled and deveined
24 6-inch flour tortillas, warmed
Pico de Gallo (page 3)
Guacamole (page 10)

Bring a very large pot of water to a boil. Stir in 2 tablespoons salt, add the lobsters, and cook them, stirring once or twice, for 10 minutes. The lobsters' tails, when straightened, should snap back in place, and the lobster meat should be almost fully cooked. Cool the lobsters to room temperature in a colander. Crack open the claws and body shell and remove the lobster meat in pieces as large as possible. *The lobsters can be cooked up to 1 day in advance. Wrap the meat and refrigerate it.*

In a food processor, working in batches if necessary, purée together the salsa, red onions, cilantro, jalapeños, tequila, lime juice, and 1 teaspoon salt. Stir in the beer. In two or three shallow nonreactive dishes, combine the lobster meat, skirt steaks, chicken breasts, and shrimp with the marinade. Cover and let them stand at room temperature, stirring once or twice, for 2 hours. Thread the shrimp on skewers.

Preheat a gas grill (medium-high) or light a charcoal fire and let it burn down until the coals are evenly white. Position the rack about 6 inches from the heat source. Lay the skirt steaks on the grill and spoon half the marinade over the meat. Lower the cover and cook 7 minutes. Turn the steaks. Lay the chicken breasts, lobster meat, and skewered shrimp on the grill, baste everything with the remaining marinade (there will be steam and smoke), and cover the grill. Cook another 7 minutes, turning the chicken breasts, lobster meat, and shrimp at the halfway point, or until the steaks are medium-rare and the chicken, shrimp, and lobster are lightly browned and cooked through.

Transfer the steaks and chicken breasts to a cutting board, tent them with foil, and let them rest 10 minutes. Keep the shrimp warm. Slice the lobster pieces about ½-inch thick and keep them warm. Carve the steak and chicken breasts across the grain and at a slight angle into ¼-inch slices. Arrange the steak, chicken, lobster, and shrimp on a warmed platter and serve immediately, accompanied by the warmed tortillas, pico de gallo, and guacamole.

serves 8

chapter five

a bowl of welcome
soups and stews

Soups soothe, comfort, and nourish.
Stews do the same, only more so. Is it any wonder that in a place where chili is
so important other similar long-cooked dishes are done with equal skill? The
foundation for many of these is the rich broth created from the simmering of meats and
poultry that end up as shredded fillings for tacos, tamales, and so on. So soups
and stews also demonstrate kitchen frugality which, along with comfort and nutrition,
is one the essential qualities of the Southwestern kitchen.

el paso gazpacho with garlic-shrimp salad

During the summer, El Paso sizzles, and it's been our experience that when it does, people yearn for light, cool, and zesty fare. (The idea that in hot weather people lose their appetites or, worse, desire bland food, is, in our opinion, loco.) This grand gazpacho is intended as a main course and will cool and satisfy a sizable crowd, even on the steamiest day of the year. Other shellfish—lobster, crab, scallops—can replace or join the shrimp.

GAZPACHO
6 long green chiles
3 pounds (6 large) red-ripe toma-
    toes, halved, seeded, and
    chopped
3 cups canned tomato juice
1 medium cucumber (about ¾
    pound), peeled, seeded, and
    chopped
1 cup chopped onion
2 4-ounce jars roasted red peppers,
    drained
⅓ cup balsamic vinegar
⅓ cup olive oil
3 tablespoons hot pepper sauce
2 tablespoons fresh lemon juice
1 tablespoon salt

GARLIC-SHRIMP SALAD
2 teaspoons salt
1½ pounds (about 36) medium
    shrimp, shelled and deveined
Peppery Garlic-Lime Mayonnaise
    (page 98)
3 green onions, trimmed and sliced
    (about ½ cup)
2 buttery-ripe black-skinned avoca-
    dos, pitted, peeled, and diced, for
    garnish (optional)

FOR THE GAZPACHO
In the open flame of a gas burner or under a preheated broiler, roast the long green chiles, turning them, until they are lightly but evenly charred. Steam the chiles in a paper bag, or in a bowl, covered with a plate, until cool. Rub away the burned peel. Stem and seed the chiles and coarsely chop them. There should be about 1 cup.

In a food processor, combine the tomatoes and about half the tomato juice and process until smooth. Transfer this to a large bowl. In the food processor, combine the remaining tomato juice, cucumber, onions, and roasted red peppers and process until smooth. Transfer this to the bowl. Stir in the balsamic vinegar, olive oil, hot pepper sauce, lemon juice, salt, and chopped green chiles. Cover and refrigerate until very cold, at least 5 hours and preferably overnight.

FOR THE SHRIMP SALAD

Bring a medium pan of water to a boil. Stir in the salt and shrimp and cook just until the shrimp are curled, pink, and opaque, about 4 minutes. Drain them immediately and cool them to room temperature.

Coarsely chop the shrimp. In a medium bowl, combine the shrimp with the mayonnaise and green onions. Adjust the seasoning.

Ladle the gazpacho into wide bowls. Spoon a generous dollop of shrimp salad into the center of each bowl of gazpacho, dividing it evenly and using it all. Scatter the diced avocados, if you are using them, around the shrimp salad and serve immediately.

serves 12

peppery garlic-lime mayonnaise

2 tablespoons lime juice
1 egg yolk, at room temperature
2 garlic cloves, peeled and minced
Grated zest of 1 lime
1 teaspoon prepared Dijon-style
    mustard

½ teaspoon freshly ground black
    pepper
¼ teaspoon salt
½ cup corn oil
⅓ cup olive oil

In a small food processor, combine 1 tablespoon of the lime juice, the egg yolk, garlic, lime zest, mustard, freshly ground black pepper, and salt. Process until smooth. With the motor running, add the corn oil and olive oil in a fairly quick, steady stream. The mayonnaise will thicken. Adjust the seasoning, adding more lime juice if desired. *The mayonnaise can be prepared up to 3 days ahead. Cover it and refrigerate.*

makes about 1 cup

clear chicken broth with shrimp, corn, and cilantro

This is an elegant approach to the various garnished broths that are dear to the Mexican diner's heart. Clarified using beaten egg whites, this rich, delicate soup is a shimmering gold, afloat with shrimp, tomatoes, corn, cilantro, and lime—a beautiful starter for an important dinner. Making it is a rather long but not difficult process, and it can be completed well in advance, in several easy stages. The final cooking and garnishing then take mere minutes.

3 tablespoons corn oil
1½ pounds chicken backs, necks, and wings
2 cups chopped onion
3 carrots, peeled and chopped
6 garlic cloves, peeled
1 teaspoon dried thyme, crumbled
1 teaspoon dried oregano, crumbled
2 bay leaves
12 whole black peppercorns
12 medium shrimp, shelled and de-veined, with the shells reserved
7 cups chicken broth, homemade or canned

2 egg whites
About ½ teaspoon salt
2 ripe Italian-style plum tomatoes, trimmed, seeded, and diced
3 green onions, trimmed and sliced (about ½ cup)
½ cup corn kernels, canned or de-frosted frozen, well drained
½ cup minced cilantro
4 paper-thin slices of lime, for garnish

In a heavy 5-quart pan over medium-high heat, warm the corn oil. Pat the chicken parts dry and, working in batches, cook them, stirring occasionally, until well browned, about 10 minutes. Reserve the chicken parts; do not clean the pan.

Set the pan over low heat. Add the onions, carrots, garlic, thyme, oregano, bay leaves, pepper-corns, and shells from the shrimp. Cover, lower the heat, and cook, stirring occasionally and scraping the browned deposits from the bottom of the pan, for 15 minutes.

Return the chicken parts to the pan. Add the chicken broth, raise the heat, and bring to a boil, skimming any scum that forms. Lower the heat, partially cover, and simmer, stirring once or twice, for 2 hours. Cool the broth slightly and strain, pressing hard on the solids with the back of a spoon to extract all the juices. Degrease the broth. Measure it and, if you have more than 5 cups, simmer it in a saucepan over high heat until it is reduced. Cool, cover, and refrigerate. *The broth can be prepared to this point 2 days ahead.*

Bring the broth to room temperature. In a medium bowl, whisk together 1 cup of the broth and the egg whites. In a medium saucepan over low heat, bring the remaining broth to a simmer. Slowly whisk the hot broth into the egg white mixture. Return the mixture to the pan and set over medium heat. Bring just to a simmer, then lower the heat and leave undisturbed for 20 minutes. Do not allow the mixture to boil. Do not stir the mixture. The egg whites will coagulate and come to the surface of the broth as a grayish foam.

Line a strainer with a double thickness of dampened cheesecloth and set the strainer over a bowl. Gently ladle the broth and egg whites into the strainer without breaking up the egg whites. Discard the egg whites and cheesecloth. *The soup can be prepared to this point 1 day ahead. Cool the clear broth to room temperature and refrigerate, covered.*

Reheat the broth to a simmer and add salt to taste. Add the shrimp and simmer until they are pink, curled, and opaque, 3 to 4 minutes. Divide the diced tomatoes, green onions, corn kernels, and cilantro among 4 wide shallow soup bowls. Ladle the broth into the bowls, dividing the shrimp evenly. Float a slice of lime in each bowl and serve immediately.

serves 4

cream of green chile soup

Our version of this wildly popular El Paso soup combines the best features of the green chile soup served at Café Central, Jaxon's, and other local eateries. It can be made any time of year, since frozen green chiles work well, but with the promise of fall and the scent of fields of ripening fresh local chiles in the air, this creamy, slightly *picante* soup becomes an urgent need. Restaurants often serve it as a starter, but we like to enjoy a big bowl of it for a simple supper after a hard day at the office.

2 corn tortillas, preferably 1 of yellow cornmeal and 1 of blue cornmeal
6 long green chiles
½ stick (4 tablespoons) unsalted butter
2 cups chopped onion
1 garlic clove, peeled and minced
½ teaspoon dried oregano, crumbled
2 bay leaves

3½ cups chicken broth, homemade or canned
1 pound (2 medium) baking potatoes, peeled and chunked
½ teaspoon salt
¼ teaspoon freshly ground black pepper
⅓ cup whipping cream
2 cups (about 8 ounces) grated Monterey Jack cheese or mozzarella cheese or a combination of both

Cut the tortillas into ¼-inch-wide strips and leave them uncovered at room temperature until they are dry and crisp, about 24 hours.

In the open flame of a gas burner or under a preheated broiler, roast the long green chiles, turning them, until they are lightly but evenly charred. Steam the chiles in a paper bag, or in a bowl, covered with a plate, until cool. Rub away the burned peel. Stem and seed the chiles and coarsely chop them. There should be about 1 cup.

In a 4-quart saucepan over low heat, melt the butter. Add the onions, garlic, oregano, and bay leaves and cook, covered, stirring once or twice, for 10 minutes. Stir in the chicken broth, potatoes, salt, and freshly ground black pepper and bring to a boil. Lower the heat and simmer, partially covered, stirring once or twice, until the potatoes are very tender, about 25 minutes.

continued

Cool the soup slightly and then force it through the medium blade of a food mill (or discard the bay leaves and purée it in a food processor). Return the soup to the pan, stir in the green chiles, and set over medium heat. Bring to a simmer and cook, uncovered, stirring occasionally, until the soup has thickened, about 15 minutes. Stir in the cream and adjust the seasoning. *The soup can be prepared up to 3 days ahead. Cool it completely and refrigerate, covered. Rewarm it over low heat, stirring often, until steaming.*

Ladle the soup into wide bowls, sprinkle the cheese over the soup, and scatter the tortilla strips over the cheese. Serve immediately.

serves 4 to 6

lunch under bill and norma's grape arbor

Norma's Iced Mango Tea with Mint (page 243)

Chiles Rellenos Fríos con Guacamole (page 194)

El Paso Gazpacho with Garlic-Shrimp Salad (page 96)
Texas Toast (page 189)

Peach Cobbler (page 210) with Heavy Cream

ham, corn, and red pepper chowder

Jalapeños add just a little excitement to this chunky, warming main-course soup. The better the ham, the better the eating, so don't stint. Serve this soup with Masa Biscuits (page 166), butter, and mesquite honey or jalapeño jelly.

½ stick (4 tablespoons) unsalted butter

½ pound firm, smoky ham, trimmed and cut into ½-inch cubes

2 cups coarsely chopped onion

2 fresh jalapeño chiles, stemmed and chopped

1 teaspoon dried thyme, crumbled

1 bay leaf

6 cups chicken broth, homemade or canned

1 pound (about 4 medium) red-skinned potatoes, scrubbed and cut into ½-inch cubes

2 large heavy sweet red peppers, stemmed, cored, and cut into ½-inch cubes

2 teaspoons salt

2 ears of sweet corn, shucked, trimmed, and sliced crosswise into ¾-inch rounds

½ cup Crema (page 254) or whipping cream

In a heavy 5-quart soup pot over medium heat, melt the butter. Add the ham and cook, stirring occasionally, until the cubes are lightly browned, 7 to 10 minutes. With a slotted spoon transfer the ham to a bowl.

Add the onions, jalapeños, thyme, and bay leaf to the butter in the pot. Lower the heat, cover the pot, and cook, stirring once or twice and scraping the browned deposits from the bottom of the pot, for 10 minutes.

Add the chicken broth. Stir in the potatoes, sweet red peppers, 2 teaspoons of salt, and the browned ham cubes. Raise the heat and bring the soup to a boil. Lower the heat, partially cover the pot, and simmer, stirring once or twice, for 25 minutes. Stir in the rounds of corn, partially cover, and cook another 7 to 10 minutes, or until the corn, potatoes, and sweet red peppers are very tender and the soup is thick. Discard the bay leaf. Stir in the crema, adjust the seasoning, and simmer another minute or two, or until heated through.

serves 6

pueblo indian–style lamb and green chile stew

Hardy sheep were among the earliest domestic livestock, and lamb stews, fired with one or more kinds of green chiles, did a great job nourishing and warming during the high desert's bitter winters. This is our version taken from the many rustic lamb ragouts that are a part of the rich Pueblo Indian history. The most economical cut of lamb to use here is the shoulder, a fairly gnarly bit of meat that includes plenty of bone and will require of the diner some hunting to locate the tender, clinging morsels of meat. For a more sophisticated—and more expensive—version for company, ask the butcher to give you 2 pounds of 1½-inch boneless cubes of lamb from the leg.

8 green chiles, preferably a combination of long green and poblano	2 teaspoons dried oregano, crumbled
5 tablespoons olive oil	4 cups beef broth, homemade or canned
2½ pounds lamb stew meat from the shoulder, in 2- by 3-inch chunks	1 35-ounce can Italian-style plum tomatoes, crushed and drained
2 cups chopped onion	1½ teaspoons salt
3 or 4 fresh jalapeño chiles, stemmed and minced	2 pounds (about 3 large) boiling potatoes, peeled and cut into 1-inch chunks
4 garlic cloves, peeled and minced	

In the open flame of a gas burner or under a preheated broiler, roast the chiles, turning them, until they are lightly but evenly charred. Steam the chiles in a paper bag, or in a bowl, covered with a plate, until cool. Rub away the burned peel. Stem and seed the chiles and cut them into ¼-inch-wide strips.

Position a rack in the lower third of the oven and preheat the oven to 350°F.

In a 5-quart nonreactive Dutch oven or flameproof casserole over medium heat, warm 2 tablespoons of the olive oil. Pat the lamb pieces dry. Working in batches, add them to the hot olive oil and cook them, turning them occasionally and adding an additional tablespoon of oil to the pan if necessary, until well browned, 7 to 10 minutes. Transfer the browned lamb to a bowl. Discard the oil but do not clean the pan.

Set the pan over low heat, add the remaining olive oil and stir in the onions, jalapeños, garlic, and oregano. Cook, covered, stirring occasionally and scraping the browned deposits from the bottom of the pan, for 10 minutes. Stir in the beef broth and tomatoes, return the lamb to the pot, and season with the salt. Bring the stew to a boil, then cover the pan and set it in the oven. Bake it 45 minutes, stirring once or twice. Stir in the potatoes and green chiles and bake, covered, another 45 minutes, stirring once or twice, or until the lamb and potatoes are very tender and the stew has thickened slightly. Adjust the seasoning and serve it very hot.

serves 6

a high mesa dinner

Pico de Gallo (page 3) with Blue Corn Tostaditas (page 32)

Pueblo Indian–Style Lamb and Green Chile Stew (page 104)
Warmed Flour Tortillas

Peach Cobbler (page 210)

caldillo of smoked brisket with green chiles

At an altitude of nearly four thousand feet, El Paso gets darned cold in winter, and when it does, our attention turns to the kitchen, where a big pot of caldillo is soon simmering away. Caldillo means "little broth," and while it can be generically applied to any kind of stew, in El Paso it has come to mean a beef and green chile stew, one quickly concocted by using leftover roast beef (or sometimes pork or lamb). Somewhere along the line, desperately hungry for caldillo and lacking any leftover pot roast, Park resorted to using a serendipitous chunk of his own home-smoked brisket—and reinvented, in our modest opinion, caldillo. Now when the hunger for caldillo strikes, we simply stop off at the Texas BBQ (1316 Texas Avenue) on our way home from work, pick up owner Kim Gomez's spectacular mesquite-smoked brisket, and our caldillo, ready in about only an hour, is utterly delicious—and worth a trip to your backyard smoker if you can't make a trip to Texas Avenue. If your green chiles are mild, you can heat up the caldillo by cooking 2 or 3 minced fresh jalapeños along with the onions.

12 long green chiles
3 tablespoons olive oil
4 cups coarsely chopped onion
1 tablespoon ground cumin
1 teaspoon dried oregano, crumbled
8 cups beef broth or chicken broth, homemade or canned
2½ pounds boiling potatoes, peeled and cut into ½-inch dice

2 cups canned crushed tomatoes with added purée
2 pounds Home Smoker Barbecue Brisket of Beef (page 76) or Texas Party Brisket (page 118) or leftover pot roast of beef, pork, or lamb, trimmed and cut into ½-inch cubes
Salt to taste

In the open flame of a gas burner or under a preheated broiler, roast the long green chiles, turning them, until they are lightly but evenly charred. Steam the chiles in a paper bag, or in a bowl, covered with a plate, until cool. Rub away the burned peel. Stem and seed the chiles and coarsely chop them. There should be about 2 cups.

In a deep pot over low heat, warm the olive oil. Add the onions, cumin, and oregano and cook, covered, stirring once or twice, for 15 minutes.

Add the broth, potatoes, tomatoes, and green chiles and bring to a boil. Lower the heat and simmer, partially covered, stirring once or twice, for 30 minutes.

Add the cubed brisket and continue to simmer until the potatoes and the meat are very tender and the stew is thick, about 15 minutes. Add salt to taste.

serves 8

caldo tlapeno

This hearty soup/stew, fired by smoky chipotles and chock-full of chicken and vegetables, is named for a region of Mexico City (Tlapan), where it is thought to have originally been a street snack. The caldo is a popular first course in some restaurants, but we find it too substantial for that and prefer to serve it as a main course on a crisp fall or winter evening. We have given the recipe with rice as the starch, but you may substitute 2 cups of cooked chick-peas (garbanzos) added to the soup when the zucchini goes in.

1 4½- to 5-pound young chicken, cut into 8 serving pieces (reserve the wings for another use)	⅓ cup raw long grain white rice
3 tablespoons olive oil	2 large zucchini (about ¾ pound total), scrubbed, trimmed, and cut into ½-inch cubes
1½ cups chopped onion	1 buttery-ripe black-skinned avocado, pitted, peeled, and chunked
3 medium carrots, peeled and diced	
8 cups chicken broth, homemade or canned	½ cup minced fresh cilantro
4 dried chipotles	Wedges of fresh lime, for garnish

Pat the chicken pieces dry. In a 5-quart soup pot over medium heat, warm 2 tablespoons of the olive oil. Working in batches, add the chicken pieces and cook them, turning them once or twice, until lightly browned, about 4 minutes per side. Transfer the chicken pieces to a plate.

Add the remaining tablespoon of olive oil to the pot and set over medium heat. Stir in the onions and carrots and cook, covered, stirring occasionally and scraping the browned deposits from the bottom of the pan, for 5 minutes. Add the chicken broth and the chipotles and bring to a simmer. Cook, partially covered, for 15 minutes.

Stir in the rice and the browned chicken pieces and bring to a simmer. Cook, partially covered, stirring once or twice, for 30 minutes. Add the zucchini and cook another 15 minutes, or until the chicken and rice are tender. *The soup can be prepared to this point 1 day ahead. Cool it completely and refrigerate, covered. Rewarm it over low heat, stirring often.*

Remove the soup from the heat, stir in the avocado and cilantro, and let it stand, covered, for 1 minute. Ladle the soup into bowls (1 chipotle in each bowl) and serve, passing wedges of lime at the table.

serves 4

soup supper

Chilled Bohemia Ale

Epazote Quesadillas (page 19)
Pico de Gallo (page 3)

Caldo Tlapeno (page 108)
Warmed Corn Tortillas

Fresh Fruit

menudo
(tripe and hominy soup stew)

This rugged, almost primitive soup/stew is said to be a good cure for *cruda* (hangover), and it is traditional, following Sunday mass, to take your own container to the nearest menudo specialist (ours is Gussie's Bakery, a tamale place just down the block) and bring it home full of hot menudo. Nothing, of course, really prevents or cures a hangover—the best way to avoid one is not to overindulge. Our Sundays, however, are always brightened by a rib-sticking bowl or two of menudo, and sometimes, when Gussie is on vacation, we even make our own. Here's how.

MENUDO
½ pound (about 24) dried red New
    Mexico chile pods
2 to 3 chiles de arbol
3 cups water
¼ cup olive oil
4 cups chopped onion
4 garlic cloves, peeled and minced
2 teaspoons dried oregano,
    crumbled
2 pounds tripe, rinsed, trimmed,
    and cut into 1-inch squares

1 2-pound bag uncooked hominy
    (posole)
6 cups beef broth, canned or
    homemade
2 teaspoons salt

GARNISH
2 cups finely chopped onion
Dried oregano
4 limes, quartered

FOR THE MENUDO
Stem the chile pods and the chiles de arbol. Slit them open (kitchen scissors work well here). Shake out as many of the seeds as possible and rinse the chiles briefly under cold running water. Tear or snip them into 1-inch pieces.

Bring the water to a boil and pour it over the chile pieces in a medium heat-proof bowl. Cover the bowl with a lid or a plate and let the chile pieces stand, stirring them once or twice, until the water is cool.

With a slotted spoon, transfer the softened chile pieces to a blender or a food processor. Process briefly, scraping down the sides. Add some of the soaking water and process again. Continue adding water, blending, and then scraping down the sides until the water has all been used and the chile purée is smooth. Transfer the purée to a strainer set over a bowl. Add 2 tablespoons hot tap water to the blender and purée briefly to rinse the blades and inside. Add this residue to the purée in the strainer. Force the chile purée through the strainer with a stiff rubber spatula, discarding any seeds and tough bits of peel remaining in the strainer. There should be about 2 cups. *The purée can be stored, well covered, in the refrigerator for up to 3 days, or frozen for up to 1 month.*

In a large heavy pot over low heat, warm the olive oil. Stir in the onions, garlic, and oregano and cook, covered, stirring once or twice, for 15 minutes. Add the tripe, hominy, and beef broth, plus additional water to cover by 4 inches. Raise the heat and bring to a boil, then lower the heat and simmer, partially covered, stirring occasionally and skimming any scum that forms, for 2½ hours. Stir in the chile purée and salt and simmer another 35 to 45 minutes, or until the menudo is thick and the tripe and hominy are tender. *The menudo can be prepared up to 3 days ahead. Cool it completely and refrigerate, covered. Rewarm it by bringing it to a simmer over low heat, stirring often.*

Ladle the menudo into warmed bowls and serve, letting each diner garnish the menudo with chopped onions, oregano, and a squeeze or two of fresh lime juice to taste.

serves 8

chapter six

texas on the hoof
beef

The image is indelible. Like a scene from *Rawhide,* hundreds, maybe thousands, of long-horned steers jostle along a dusty trail. Every American who has ever been to the movies (or signed up for cable) knows these cattle are headed north to Abilene, and market points beyond. As good beef remains for many a national obsession, so Texas endures as the mythical heart of Cattle Country. This is more than symbolic, however. Texas really does raise much of the country's beef, and Texans esteem and prepare beef with as much, if not more, skill than cooks anywhere else in the world. The Kerrs are no exception to the Texas/beef connection, and on the following pages are some of our cherished family favorites, along with a few new recipes. From the Sunday brisket to a gravy-smothered chicken-fried steak, and from a chile-spiked meat loaf to a sizzling skillet of fajitas, this chapter is our answer to the question "Where's the beef?"

winter fajitas

These indoor fajitas are for the dead of winter, when the grill is buried under a snowdrift, or for any time, really, when you just don't want to cook outdoors. This marinade is slightly different from the one we use for our grilled fajitas (page 92)—it boosts the flavor with chipotles and liquid smoke flavoring to make up for the lack of an open flame. Cook these in one or two heavy cast-iron skillets or on a large ridged cast-iron grill pan that will fit across two burners. (Those cute little fajita skillets that come with a wood or wicker holder are useless for cooking on, but two or three can be preheated and used as serving pieces.) Be sure to turn off the smoke alarm before setting out to make this recipe.

1 cup tomato-based bottled hot salsa
½ cup chopped red onion
½ cup packed fresh cilantro (stems can be used)
¼ cup olive oil
3 chipotles adobado, with clinging sauce
2 tablespoons tequila
2 tablespoons fresh lime juice
1 tablespoon liquid hickory smoke flavoring
½ cup amber beer, such as Dos Equis

2½ to 3 pounds skirt steak, cut into 8-inch sections
Nonstick cooking spray
1 large onion (about 1 pound), peeled, halved, and cut into thin slices
2 large heavy sweet red peppers, stemmed, cored, and cut into julienne strips
½ teaspoon salt
18 6-inch flour tortillas, warmed
Pico de Gallo (page 3)
Guacamole (page 10)

In a food processor, purée the salsa, red onions, cilantro, 2 tablespoons of the olive oil, the chipotles, tequila, lime juice, and liquid smoke. Stir in the beer. In a shallow nonreactive dish, pour the marinade over the skirt steak and let it stand at room temperature, covered, turning it once or twice, for 2 hours.

Heat one or two heavy cast-iron skillets or a cast-iron stove-top grill pan over medium-high heat. When they are very hot, lightly coat the skillets with nonstick cooking spray. Letting the excess marinade drip off, and working in batches if necessary, place the meat in the skillets. Cook, turning once or twice, until browned on the outside and medium-rare inside, 4 to 5 minutes per side. Transfer the meat to a cutting board and let it rest for 10 minutes.

Meanwhile, in a large heavy skillet over medium heat, warm the remaining 2 tablespoons of olive oil. Stir in the onions and sweet red peppers, season with salt, and cook, covered, stirring once or twice, for 8 minutes.

Cut the meat, across the grain and at a slight angle, into thin slices. Add the meat and any juices from the cutting board to the skillet with the onions and peppers. Raise the heat to high and cook uncovered, tossing and stirring, until the meat is heated through and the onions and peppers are lightly browned, about 5 minutes. Transfer to heated fajita pans or a large heated platter and serve immediately, accompanied by warmed tortillas, pico de gallo, and guacamole.

serves 6

chicken-fried steak with cream gravy
and mashed potatoes

Aside from chili (and maybe politics), Texans are more likely to argue about the proper way to chicken-fry a steak than about any other crucial issue of our times. This is a little-known fact, but true, and here is our contribution to the brouhaha. We're of beaten-egg-and-cracker-crumb persuasion (there are also the buttermilk people, and the beer batter folks, plus the deep-fry school, as well as a host of splinter groups). Ours is the simplest, which means less actual time elapses between getting the steak home and cutting into it (partnered with plenty of creamy gravy and a mountain of mashed spuds). When it comes to chicken-fried steak, we have learned speedy gratification is what it's all about. This recipe produces enough gravy to cover both the steaks and the mashed potatoes, which is absolutely essential to the success of the dish.

1¾ to 2 pounds round steak, cut about ½-inch thick and tenderized by the butcher
Salt
Freshly ground black pepper
¾ cup unbleached all-purpose flour
2 eggs beaten with 1 tablespoon hot pepper sauce

6 ounces (about 4 cups) coarsely crushed saltine crackers
¼ cup corn oil
4 cups milk
1 recipe Perfectly Lumpy Mashed Potatoes (page 184)

Season each steak on both sides with a pinch of salt and of freshly ground black pepper, rubbing them into the meat. One at a time, dredge the steaks in the flour, then in the egg, then in the cracker crumbs. Reserve ¼ cup of the flour.

In a large heavy skillet over medium heat, warm the corn oil. Add the steaks and cook them, turning them carefully once or twice, until the meat is fully cooked through and the crumb coating is brown and crisp, 8 to 10 minutes total. Transfer them to a platter and keep them warm.

Pour all but 4 tablespoons of the fat in the skillet through a strainer and discard it. Return any cracklings from the strainer to the skillet and set it over low heat. Whisk the reserved ¼ cup of flour into the fat in the skillet and cook over low heat, stirring and scraping, for 2 minutes. Gradually whisk in the milk. Raise the heat slightly and bring the gravy to a simmer. Cook, stirring often and scraping the browned deposits from the bottom of the skillet, until the gravy has thickened, 5 to 6 minutes. Adjust the seasoning.

Arrange steaks on each of 4 plates. Spoon the mashed potatoes next to the steaks and nap both generously with gravy. Serve immediately.

serves 4

a texas diner supper

Classic Nachos (page 26)

Chicken-Fried Steak with Cream Gravy and Mashed Potatoes (page 116)
Calico Corn (page 182)
Texas Toast (page 189)

Grandma Lora Belle Godwin's Lemon-Buttermilk Pie (page 214)

texas party brisket

Between the brisket eaten by Texans and the brisket turned into corned beef for New Yorkers, it's a wonder there's any left over for the rest of the country. You may need to order the meat for this recipe from the butcher, but rest assured it's worth the trouble. Everybody in El Paso makes some version of this at some time or other—it's utterly easy, tender, and delicious, and duplicates (sort of) a real barbecued brisket from a real smokehouse. Sometimes we serve this like good old American pot roast with potatoes and all the trimmings; sometimes we accompany it with coleslaw and potato salad, passing a warmed jar of our Tequila Barbecue Sauce at the table; and other times we choose Mexican accompaniments for it, rolling the brisket slices into tortillas and garnishing them just like fajitas.

1 13¾-ounce can beef broth or homemade	1 tablespoon tomato paste
1 4-ounce bottle liquid smoke	Flour
¼ cup Worcestershire sauce	1 5-pound top-cut brisket of beef
1 tablespoon dark brown sugar	1 large onion, peeled and sliced
1 tablespoon hot pepper sauce	3 garlic cloves, peeled and minced

In a medium bowl, whisk together the beef broth, liquid smoke, Worcestershire sauce, brown sugar, hot pepper sauce, and tomato paste.

Pierce and flour a large (holding up to 12 pounds) brown-in-bag according to the manufacturer's directions. Lay the brisket, fat-side up, in the bag and put the bag in a shallow baking dish just large enough to hold it. Scatter the onion slices and garlic over the brisket. Pour the broth mixture over the brisket and seal the bag. Let it stand at room temperature for 1 hour.

Position a rack in the middle of the oven and preheat the oven to 325°F. Bake the brisket about 4 hours, or until it is very tender. Then let it rest in the bag on a rack for 10 minutes.

Transfer the brisket to a cutting board, discarding the onion slices and liquid. Carve it, across the grain and at a slight angle, into thin slices. Serve immediately.

serves 8

border brisket supper

Chilled Corona Beer with Lime

**Texas Party Brisket (page 118) with Flour Tortillas and Pico de Gallo (page 3)
and Mantequilla de los Pobres (page 11)
Frijoles Negros de Olla (page 179)
Texmati Pilaf (page 181)**

Forti's Almond Flan (page 234)

salpicón
(shredded beef salad with chipotle dressing)

If there is a single dish of food that epitomizes El Paso for us, it is this unique beef salad. A genuine local speciality, it is at once smoky and tart, cool and spicy, meaty and light. Rolled up in warmed 3-inch corn or flour tortillas, it's a great cocktail buffet dish; in restaurants it goes into the center of the table as a communal appetizer; and for company meals at home—particularly during hot weather—it can be eaten with a fork as a great, individually plated main course. Julio's in Juárez and Rubio's in El Paso both make exemplary versions which we have used (aided by some sound advice from local caterer Kay Queveda) as the inspiration for this recipe. The finished platter in this recipe is festive enough, but for a really grand presentation, omit the rajas and avocado wedges and garnish the salpicón with guacamole-stuffed fire-roasted long green chiles (page 194). (As a bonus, this recipe produces spectacular beef broth—be sure to save it for another use.)

1 5-pound top-cut brisket of beef
2 large onions, peeled and sliced
1 quart beef broth, canned
4 poblano chiles or 6 long green
   chiles
1 7-ounce can chipotles adobado,
   puréed
⅔ cup olive oil
½ cup fresh lime juice
⅓ cup white wine vinegar
1½ teaspoons salt
2 garlic cloves, crushed through a
   press
8 ounces mild white cheese, such as
   Monterey Jack, cut into ¼-inch dice

1 cup coarsely diced red onion
¾ cup minced cilantro
1 head of romaine, separated into
   leaves, for garnish
3 medium tomatoes, trimmed and
   cut into wedges, for garnish
2 buttery-ripe black-skinned avocados, pitted and cut into thin
   wedges (do not peel), for garnish
5 radishes, trimmed and sliced into
   paper-thin rounds, for garnish
Small corn or flour tortillas,
   warmed (optional)

Lay the brisket, fat-side up, in a 6-quart Dutch oven or flameproof casserole. Scatter the onion slices over the meat. Pour in the beef broth and add cold water to cover the brisket by 3 inches. Set over medium heat and bring to a boil. Cover, lower the heat, and simmer, adding additional boiling water as necessary and turning the brisket at the approximate halfway point, until it is tender enough to shred easily at its thickest point, about 4 hours total cooking time. Remove it from the heat, uncover the pan, and let the brisket stand in the broth until it is just cool enough to handle. (Warm brisket is easier to shred.)

Meanwhile, in the open flame of a gas burner or under a preheated broiler, roast the chiles, turning them, until they are lightly but evenly charred. Steam the chiles in a paper bag, or in a bowl, covered with a plate, until cool. Rub away the burned peel. Stem and seed the chiles and cut them into ¼-inch-wide strips.

Pour off and strain the broth. Measure out 1½ cups, reserving the remainder for another use. Trim the fat from the brisket, and using the tines of two forks, one in each hand, in a downward pulling motion, *thoroughly* shred the meat. (The results should be almost fluffy.)

In a bowl, combine the shredded beef and the broth and let stand, covered, at room temperature. *The meat can be prepared to this point up to 2 hours ahead. Do not refrigerate.*

In a medium bowl, whisk together the puréed chipotles, olive oil, lime juice, vinegar, salt, and garlic.

Drain the shredded meat, pressing hard with a spoon to extract any broth that has not been absorbed. In a large bowl, toss together the shredded beef, diced cheese, and chipotle mixture. Add the red onions, cilantro, and chile strips and toss again. Taste and adjust the seasoning (the salpicón should be tart, smoky, and fairly *picante*).

Line a large platter with the coarse outer leaves of the romaine. Mound the salpicón on the lettuce. Garnish with the spiky yellow inner leaves of the romaine, the tomatoes, and avocado wedges. Scatter the radish rounds over all and serve, accompanied, if desired, by warmed tortillas.

serves 12 as a main course, 20 or more as an hors d'oeuvre

a cool cocktail party

Park's Easy Frozen Margaritas (page 239)
White Sangria (page 241)
A Big Tub of Beers on Ice

Assorted Salsas (except Tropical Mango Salsa) (pages 3–7)
Guacamole (page 10) with Tostaditas (page 32) and Wedges of Jicama

Salpicón (page 120) with Corn Tortillas

A Dessert Tray of Pineapple-Apricot Empanaditas (page 224), Bizcochos (page 220),
and Fresh Strawberries

tex-mex chili-cheese meat loaf

This meat loaf is just as flavorful and zesty as a bowl of good chili. Serve it with Texmati Pilaf (page 181) and Calico Corn (page 182) or with Perfectly Lumpy Mashed Potatoes (page 184) and Calabacitas con Crema (page 185). And be sure to save a slice or two for making sandwiches the next day.

3 tablespoons olive oil
1 cup finely chopped onion
1 large heavy sweet red pepper, stemmed, cored, and finely chopped
2 to 3 fresh jalapeño chiles, stemmed and minced
2 garlic cloves, peeled and minced
2 tablespoons mild chili powder blend
2 teaspoons salt
1½ teaspoons oregano, crumbled
1½ teaspoons ground cumin

1 28-ounce can Italian-style plum tomatoes, crushed and drained
1½ pounds ground beef, not too lean
½ pound ground pork, not too lean
1 cup fine, dry (commercially prepared) bread crumbs
2 eggs, beaten
1 cup canned or defrosted frozen corn kernels, well drained
3 green onions, trimmed and sliced (about ½ cup)
8 ounces medium-sharp cheddar cheese, grated

Position a rack in the lower third of the oven and preheat the oven to 350°F.

In a medium skillet over moderate heat, warm the olive oil. Add the onions, sweet red pepper, jalapeños, garlic, chili powder blend, salt, oregano, and cumin. Cover, lower the heat, and cook, stirring once or twice, for 10 minutes. Add the tomatoes and cook, covered, stirring once or twice, for 10 minutes. Remove from the heat and cool to room temperature.

In a large bowl, combine the beef and pork. Add the tomato mixture, bread crumbs, and eggs and mix thoroughly (hands work best). Add the corn and green onions and mix well. Transfer the meat mixture to a shallow baking dish and form it into a flat loaf. Bake about 1 hour and 20 minutes, or until an instant-reading thermometer inserted into the center of the loaf registers 160°F.

Pour off any fat from the dish. Sprinkle the cheese evenly over the meat loaf and return it to the oven until the cheese is just melted, about 4 minutes. Serve immediately.

serves 8

chili joes

In west Texas even the kids like it hot. Witness the enduring popularity of these childishly sloppy sandwiches, which have appeared regularly on the Kerr family table for years. Once a reliable and convenient workday supper, they're now nostalgic comfort food. We use our Snakebite Salsa and our special El Paso chile seasoning blend, and while we understandably feel this results in a superior sandwich, supermarket salsas and chili powders also make great sloppy eating. (For a milder "Joe," just use a milder salsa.)

3 tablespoons olive oil
1½ cups chopped onion
1 large heavy sweet red pepper, stemmed, cored, and finely diced
3 garlic cloves, peeled and minced
4 teaspoons chili powder blend
1 teaspoon oregano, crumbled
½ teaspoon ground cumin
Pinch of cinnamon
2 pounds lean ground beef
1½ teaspoons salt

1½ cups thick tomato-based bottled salsa, mild or hot
½ cup water
1 10½-ounce can dark red kidney beans, drained and rinsed
⅓ cup minced cilantro
6 large firm sandwich buns, such as Kaiser rolls, split
6 ounces medium-sharp cheddar cheese, sliced

In a large skillet over low heat, warm the olive oil. Add the onions, sweet red pepper, garlic, chili powder blend, oregano, cumin, and cinnamon and cook, covered, stirring once or twice, for 10 minutes.

Add the ground beef, breaking it up with a fork, and the salt and cook, stirring often, until the meat is no longer pink, about 12 minutes. Stir in the salsa and water and bring to a boil. Partially cover, lower the heat, and simmer, stirring once or twice, until very thick, about 50 minutes. Stir in the beans. *The mixture can be prepared up to 3 days ahead. Cool it and refrigerate, covered. Rewarm it slowly over low heat, stirring often.*

Preheat the broiler. Stir the cilantro into the meat mixture and adjust the seasoning.

Lightly toast the sandwich buns, cut-sides up, under the broiler. Arrange the cheese slices on the toasted tops of the buns and return them to the broiler until the cheese is just melted.

Spoon the meat mixture onto the bottoms of the buns, cover with the tops, and serve immediately.

makes 6 sandwiches

a weekday supper

Ice-cold Milk

Chili Joes (page 124)
Jalapeño-Pineapple Coleslaw (page 199)
Tostaditas (page 32)

Crisp Apples

chapter seven

qwit yer beefin'
pork, lamb, and game

Besides beef, Texans also cook up plenty of other meat. Pork products are highly regarded in Texas, for example, especially by those of us in west Texas who live under the influence of Old Mexico. There the hard-foraging, low-maintenance pig is regarded even above the cow, and the number of delicious things possible is mind-boggling. And remember the Saturday matinee ranchers and sheepherders shooting it out in the sagebrush? The herders seem to have won the battle, for there are plenty of sheep raised and cooked in Texas nowadays. From the backyard grill to the roadside taco stand, many wonderful Southwestern dishes let lamb shine. And think again of the old movies in which wagon trains moved slowly west, foraging and hunting as they crossed the wild country. That tradition, too, persists in Texas, and while hunting is now mostly an expensive hobby for a few, rather than a frugal necessity for many, modern Texans cook farm-raised game with skill based on generations of practice. From a grandly glazed ham, to a breakfast skillet of bacon-wrapped quail, and on to mellow pheasant potpie and fiery chile-marinated spareribs, this chapter contains a mixed bag of (non-beef) family classics with modern appeal.

baked spareribs in honey-orange adobo

The ribs marinate in the adobo—a thick paste of chili powder, orange peel, and honey—for twenty-four hours before being slowly baked to spicy tenderness. Use meaty "regular" ribs, not baby backs, for the proper succulence.

⅔ cup chili powder blend
½ cup fresh orange juice
¼ cup olive oil
2 tablespoons fresh lime juice
3 medium garlic cloves, peeled and
  crushed through a press
4 teaspoons ground cumin
1 tablespoon minced orange zest

1 tablespoon honey
1 tablespoon tomato paste
2 teaspoons dried oregano,
  crumbled
2 teaspoons salt
6 pounds spareribs, chine bones
  cracked for easier serving

In a small bowl, stir together the chili powder blend, orange juice, olive oil, lime juice, garlic, cumin, orange zest, honey, tomato paste, oregano, and 1½ teaspoons of salt.

With a sharp knife, slash a shallow crosshatch pattern into the meaty side of the ribs. Lay the ribs in a single layer in a large shallow baking pan. Spread the paste over both sides of the ribs, rubbing it well into the crosshatching. Cover the pan and refrigerate the ribs for at least 24 and up to 48 hours.

Position a rack in the upper third of the oven and preheat the oven to 350°F. Bake them, meaty-side down, for 30 minutes. Turn the ribs over and bake them another 35 to 45 minutes, covering them loosely with foil if the adobo gets too brown, or until they are tender.

Transfer the ribs to a cutting board and let them rest, tented with foil, for 10 minutes. With a thin sharp knife, cut the ribs apart and serve immediately.

serves 4

pork deshebrada
(shredded pork)

This is the recipe for the braised, shredded pork that serves as a filling for tamales, tamale pie, street tacos, and so on. The recipe produces as well a generous quantity of red chile pork broth, which adds ruddy color and flavor to those fillings. The amount of shredded pork from this recipe is considerable, but it freezes well, moistened with a bit of the braising liquid, for up to three months.

½ pound (about 24) large dried red
    New Mexico chile pods (page 250)
4 to 5 chiles de arbol
3 cups water
1 6½- to 7-pound bone-in pork
    shoulder roast (*calas*)
2 medium onions, peeled and sliced

3 garlic cloves, peeled and minced
5 cups chicken broth, homemade or
    canned
2 teaspoons dried oregano,
    crumbled
2 teaspoons ground cumin
2 teaspoons salt

Stem the chile pods and the chiles de arbol. Slit them open (kitchen scissors work well here). Shake out as many of the seeds as possible and rinse the pods briefly under cold running water. Tear or snip them into 1-inch pieces.

Bring the water to a boil and pour it over the chile pieces in a medium heat-proof bowl. Cover the bowl with a lid or a plate and let the chile pieces stand, stirring them once or twice, until the water is cool.

With a slotted spoon, transfer the softened chile pieces to a blender or a food processor. Process briefly, scraping down the sides. Add some of the soaking water and process again. Continue adding water, blending, and then scraping down the sides until the water has all been used and the chile purée is smooth. Transfer the purée to a strainer set over a bowl. Add 2 tablespoons hot tap water to the blender and purée briefly, to rinse the blades and the inside. Add this residue to the purée in the strainer. Force the puréed chiles through the strainer with a stiff rubber spatula, discarding any seeds and tough bits of peel remaining in the strainer. *The purée can be stored, well covered, in the refrigerator for up to 3 days, or frozen for up to 1 month.*

Position a rack in the lower third of the oven and preheat the oven to 375°F.

Lay the pork shoulder fat-side up in a heavy 8-quart flameproof Dutch oven. Scatter the onion slices and garlic over the roast. Pour the chile purée and chicken broth over the roast. Add enough water (about 4 cups) to bring the liquid halfway up the side of the roast. Stir in the oregano, cumin, and salt. Set the pan over medium heat, cover, and bring the liquid to a simmer. Put the roast in the oven and cook it, covered, turning it once at the estimated halfway point, for about 5 hours, or until the meat is very tender.

Cool the pork in its braising liquid, in the pan set on a rack, to room temperature. Transfer it to a cutting board, trim away any fat, and remove the bone. Using the tines of two forks, one held in each hand, in a downward pulling motion, shred the meat. Strain and degrease the broth. *The pork can be prepared up to 3 days ahead and refrigerated, or up to 3 months ahead and frozen. Moisten the meat with a cup or so of the broth. Store the meat and the remaining broth separately.*

makes about 10 cups

pepper jelly–glazed ham

Sweet and hot pepper jelly (our product or another) provides an attractive glaze and a touch of piquant heat when basted over a smoky ham as it bakes. Ham is one of our favorite main courses for a big Sunday dinner, as well as the frequent star of a groaning holiday buffet. Use a bone-in, fully cooked brine-cured "city" ham, as opposed to the stronger, saltier Smithfield type. The leftovers turn up in sandwiches, omelets, and lunch boxes; the bone is used for soups.

1 18- to 20-pound brine-cured ham   1 cup orange or apple juice
1 cup jalapeño jelly

Remove the ham from the refrigerator about 3½ hours before serving time to let it come to room temperature. If the upper surface is covered with a rind, pull it away with your fingers. With a thin sharp knife, slice away the thick layer of fat beneath the rind until only about ¼ inch remains. Score a diamond pattern about ½-inch deep into the upper surface of the ham with the knife.

Position a rack in the lower third of the oven and preheat the oven to 325°F.

Set the ham in a large shallow baking dish or in a jelly roll pan. Put it on the oven rack, add 1 cup water to the pan, and bake for 1½ hours. Meanwhile, in a small saucepan over low heat, melt the jalapeño jelly.

Pour off the water from the roasting pan, replace it with the orange juice, and continue to bake the ham, basting it every 10 minutes, first with the melted jalapeño jelly and then with the accumulated juices from the pan, until it is golden brown and shiny and is fully heated through, about 40 minutes.

Let the ham rest at least 20 minutes before carving it. Serve warm or cool.

serves 12, with leftovers

a holiday buffet

Rio Grande Lemonade (page 242)

Texas Trash (page 17)
Guacamole (page 10) with Jicama Wedges
Blue Corn Nachos with Bacon and Sweet Onions (page 28)

Apple-Marinated Hickory-Smoked Turkey Breast (page 82)
Pepper Jelly–Glazed Ham (page 132)
Edythe May's Mango Salad (page 198)
Roasted New Potato Salad with Green Chiles (page 201)

"Aunt Hazel Millican's" Sweet Chocolate Cake (page 208)
Dulces (page 235)
Pineapple-Apricot Empanaditas (page 224)

spice-coated grilled leg of lamb

A butterflied leg of lamb is pretty rough-looking ("caveman meat," according to one food writer), but it's simple to grill and to carve and the uneven thickness means there is lamb ranging from almost well-done to medium-rare—useful for pleasing everyone in the crowd. This easy recipe is adapted from Michael's cookbook *The New American Kitchen*.

2 medium onions, peeled and
  chopped
6 garlic cloves, peeled and chopped
3 fresh jalapeño chiles, stemmed
  and chopped
½ cup olive oil
⅓ cup fresh lime juice
3½ tablespoons chili powder blend

1 tablespoon ground cumin
1 tablespoon dried oregano,
  crumbled
2 teaspoons salt
1 boneless butterflied leg of lamb
  (about 7 pounds after boning)
3 cups mesquite or hickory wood
  smoking chips

In a food processor, combine the onions, garlic, and jalapeños and process until almost smooth. Add the olive oil, lime juice, chili powder blend, cumin, oregano, and salt and process until smooth. In a large nonreactive bowl, pour the purée over the lamb. Cover and refrigerate 24 hours, turning the meat occasionally. Bring the lamb to room temperature.

Soak the wood chips in water to cover for at least 30 minutes.

Preheat a gas grill (medium) or light a charcoal fire and let it burn down until the coals are evenly white. Drain the wood chips and scatter them over the coals or grill stones. Position the rack about 6 inches from the heat source and cover the grill. When the chips are smoking, lay the lamb on the grill and cook it, covered, turning it occasionally and basting it with the remaining purée, until the thickest portions of the meat are medium-rare, about 50 minutes.

Transfer the lamb to a cutting board, tent it with foil, and let it rest for 10 minutes. Carve the meat across the grain and at a slight angle into thin slices. Serve hot or warm.

serves 8 to 10

red meat on the grill

Pheasant Ridge Texas Cabernet Sauvignon Lubbock County

Pico de Gallo (page 3) with Tostaditas (page 32)
Queso Fundido on the Grill (page 20) with Warm Corn Tortillas

Spice-Coated Grilled Leg of Lamb (page 134)
Grilled Vegetable Platter (page 186)
Frijoles Negros de Olla (page 179)
Texas Toast (page 189)

Tequila-Drizzled Pear and Cactus Pear Ice (page 233) with Sliced Fresh Mangoes

tame game

There is an enormous amount of guesswork involved in cooking wild game. We admire those who are experts, but we have often been disappointed by a lengthy preparation that resulted in a game dish that was tough, strong, or otherwise inedible. (We wonder how many devotees grimly chomp through such fare, determined to get a return on the time spent hunting and cooking it.) It's a relief to report that farm-raised game is increasingly available, much of it with almost the same rich flavor as wild game, but with a great deal of the uncertainty removed. This tame game is much more tender, arrives in good condition, free for the most part of buckshot and other dental perils, and is a real pleasure to cook and to eat. (Such game is not, however, inexpensive and, except for certain gourmet markets in larger cities, is not readily available except by mail order.) Though there is a long and honorable Texas tradition of hunting and enjoying the results of the hunt at the table, we endorse cultivated game whole-heartedly, and have tested—and enjoyed—these recipes accordingly.

quail with bacon

Quail season is a fine time to be out tramping the countryside, and bagging enough of these tiny birds to prepare this recipe is the hunter's reward. Wild quail benefit from a brief marination in white wine, garlic, and olive oil; farm-raised birds require no such special handling and can be wrapped in bacon and sizzling away in a skillet almost as soon as you get home from the store. The results are delicious for dinner, spectacular at breakfast, and even without the savory smells of woodsmoke and a simmering pot of strong, bourbon-laced campfire coffee, you'll think you're in west Texas on a crisp December day.

8 domestically raised quail (about 5 ounces each), dressed
8 thick slices (about ¾ pound) premium bacon, preferably mesquite-smoked or black pepper–coated

1 cup unbleached all-purpose flour
2 teaspoons salt
2 teaspoons freshly ground black pepper
1 teaspoon dried thyme, crumbled
¼ cup olive oil

With poultry shears, split each quail down the back; discard the necks. Open each bird slightly and flatten it with the palm of your hand, cracking the breastbone as you do so. Wrap each quail in a slice of bacon, securing the ends together on the bony side of the birds with a toothpick.

In a shallow pan (like a pie plate), combine the flour, salt, freshly ground black pepper, and thyme. Dredge the quail in the flour and shake off the excess. In each of two large skillets over medium heat, warm half the olive oil. When it is hot, add the quail, meaty-side up, and cook 4 minutes. Turn the quail and cook 7 minutes. Turn the quail again, cover the pan, and cook another 3 to 4 minutes, or until the quail are fully cooked and the bacon is crisp and browned. Remove the toothpicks, transfer the quail to plates, and serve immediately.

serves 4

pan-fried rabbit with salsa-mustard sauce

Moist, flavorful rabbit is the most readily available of the nonferal game meats, found in the freezer case of many supermarkets. Fresh rabbit is better than frozen, but frozen rabbit is certainly better than no rabbit at all, especially when fried up crisp and napped with a creamy pan sauce. (We were thrilled to find two of our favorite condiments—salsa and mustard—so beautifully compatible with rabbit.) Mashed potatoes are the ideal accompaniment.

2 domestically raised young rabbits, preferably fresh (about 3 pounds each), dressed

1½ cups cultured buttermilk

1 tablespoon hot pepper sauce

2 garlic cloves, crushed through a press

1½ cups plus 3 tablespoons unbleached all-purpose flour

½ teaspoon salt

½ teaspoon freshly ground black pepper

About 2 pounds solid vegetable shortening

2 cups chicken broth, homemade or canned

½ cup tomato-based bottled hot salsa

½ cup Crema (page 254) or crème fraîche

1 tablespoon prepared Dijon-style mustard

Remove the front and hind legs from the rabbits. Remove the first (smaller) section of each front leg and reserve for another use. Cut away and discard the rib cage and the flap of belly meat on each rabbit. Cut the loin section of each rabbit in half crosswise.

In a nonreactive dish, combine the 12 rabbit pieces with the buttermilk, hot pepper sauce, and garlic. Cover and let stand at room temperature, stirring once or twice for 2 hours.

In a wide shallow dish (like a pie plate), stir together 1½ cups of the flour, the salt, and freshly ground black pepper. One at a time, remove the rabbit pieces from the marinade, letting most of it drip off, dredge them in the seasoned flour, and transfer them to a rack.

In each of two large skillets over medium heat, melt enough shortening to make it about 1-inch deep. When it is very hot, lay the rabbit pieces carefully in the shortening. Cook them, turning them once at the approximate halfway point, until the pieces are crisp and brown outside, fully cooked but still moist within, about 14 minutes total. Transfer them to absorbent paper and keep warm.

Reserve 3 tablespoons of the cooking fat. Pour the remaining fat through a strainer; return any cracklings from the strainer to one of the two skillets and set it over low heat. Scrape any cracklings from the other skillet into the skillet over low heat. Whisk the remaining 3 tablespoons of flour into the fat and cook, stirring and scraping, for 3 minutes. Whisk in the chicken broth, salsa, and crema and bring to a simmer. Cook, stirring and scraping, until the sauce has thickened, about 5 minutes. Whisk the mustard into the sauce, adjust the seasoning, and serve, spooning the sauce over the rabbit pieces.

serves 6 to 8

smothered doves

The title of this recipe refers to the cooking method, not some cruel hunting practice, and in this recipe the birds are slowly braised in a rich red chile sauce, which is thickened with cornmeal and spooned over them like gravy just before serving. The doves sought by sportsmen in Texas are turtledoves; the farm-raised version is squab, or young pigeon. The meat is dark and liverish, and is perfectly complemented by the potent, brick-colored sauce. There is lots of it, by the way; serve the squabs on top of a mound of white rice and pass plenty of flour tortillas for the mopping-up operation.

12 dried red chile pods (about ¼
   pound), preferably including 2
   or 3 anchos
1½ cups water
4 domestically raised squabs (about
   14 ounces each), dressed
3 tablespoons olive oil
2 cups chopped onion
2 garlic cloves, peeled and minced
1 tablespoon unsweetened cocoa
   powder

1 teaspoon dried oregano, crumbled
1 teaspoon ground cumin
¼ teaspoon ground cinnamon
2 bay leaves
1½ cups chicken broth, homemade
   or canned
½ teaspoon salt
2 to 3 tablespoons yellow cornmeal,
   preferably stone-ground

Stem the red chile pods and the anchos if you are using them. Slit the chiles open (kitchen scissors work well here). Shake out as many of the seeds as possible and rinse the chiles briefly under cold running water. Tear or snip them into 1-inch pieces.

Bring the water to a boil and pour it over the chile pieces in a medium heat-proof bowl. Cover the bowl with a lid or a plate and let the chile pieces stand, stirring them once or twice, until the water is cool.

With a slotted spoon, transfer the softened chile pieces to the jar of a blender or the work bowl of a food processor. Process briefly, scraping down the sides. Add some of the soaking water and process again. Continue adding water, blending, and then scraping down the sides until the water has all been used and the chile purée is smooth. Transfer the purée to a strainer set over a bowl. Add 2 tablespoons hot tap water to the blender and purée briefly, to rinse the blades and sides of the jar. Add this residue to the purée in the strainer. Force the chile purée through the strainer with a stiff rubber spatula, discarding any seeds and tough bits of peel remaining in the strainer. There should be about 1¼ cups purée. If there is more, use it all. If there is less, soak, simmer, and purée additional chiles. *The purée can be stored, well covered, in the refrigerator for up to 3 days, or frozen for up to 1 month.*

With poultry shears or a long sharp knife, cut each squab in half; discard the necks. Pat the squabs dry. In a large skillet that will just hold the squabs in a single layer, warm the olive oil over medium heat. Working in batches, add the squabs and cook them, turning them once, until well browned, about 7 minutes per side. Transfer the squabs to a plate.

To the fat in the skillet, add the onions, garlic, cocoa powder, oregano, cumin, cinnamon, and bay leaves. Lower the heat, cover the skillet, and cook, stirring once or twice, for 15 minutes. Stir in the chicken broth, chile purée, and salt. Return the squabs to the skillet. Bring the liquid to a simmer, then cover the pan. Cook the squabs, turning them twice, for about 30 minutes, or until they are tender.

Transfer the squabs to a heated platter and keep them warm. Strain the sauce into a medium saucepan, discarding the solids. Set the saucepan over medium heat and bring the sauce to a boil. Cook hard, stirring often, for 5 minutes. Lower the heat until the sauce simmers and whisk in the cornmeal, 1 tablespoon at a time, until the sauce has thickened slightly and any surface fat has been absorbed, about 4 minutes. Adjust the seasoning. Serve the squabs napped with the sauce.

serves 4

pheasant and vegetable potpie

This corn bread–topped dish was originally developed to make use of pheasants that, hit in the body instead of the head by less-than-accurate huntsmen (no names please), were too riddled with buckshot to be served whole. Over the years it's become a family favorite, one we have adapted here to make on purpose, using purchased, free-range pheasants. The combination of luxury meat and a homey presentation is an excellent example of the sophisticated but casual home entertaining we enjoy most— whether as hosts or guests.

2 domestically raised pheasants (about 3 pounds each), dressed
6 cups chicken broth, homemade or canned
2 bay leaves
12 whole black peppercorns
1 large heavy sweet red pepper
5 tablespoons unsalted butter
1 cup finely chopped onion
¼ teaspoon dried thyme, crumbled

6 tablespoons unbleached all-purpose flour
½ teaspoon salt
½ teaspoon freshly ground black pepper
¾ cup corn kernels, canned or defrosted frozen, well drained
¾ cup petite peas, defrosted frozen, well drained
Batter for 1 recipe Good Old Corn Bread (page 191)

Pick over the pheasants, removing any pinfeathers. With poultry shears or a long sharp knife, cut away the backbone of each pheasant. Quarter each pheasant. Arrange the quarters in a deep skillet just large enough to accommodate the quarters in a single layer. Pour the chicken broth over the pheasant, stir in the bay leaves and peppercorns, and set the skillet over medium heat. Bring the broth to a simmer, cover the skillet, and cook, turning the pheasant quarters once, for about 35 minutes, or until just cooked through. Cool the pheasant quarters in the broth to room temperature. Remove the skin, bones, and tendons and cut the pheasant meat into ½-inch chunks. Strain and degrease the pheasant stock (there should be about 8 cups). Transfer the stock to a medium saucepan, set over moderate heat, and bring to a brisk simmer. Cook hard, skimming occasionally, until the stock is reduced to 4 cups, about 25 minutes. *The recipe can be prepared to this point 1 day ahead. Cool the stock to room temperature, pour it over the diced pheasant, and refrigerate, covered. Return it to room temperature and pour it through a strainer, separating the meat and stock.*

In the open flame of a gas burner, or under a preheated broiler, roast the sweet red pepper, turning it, until the peel is evenly charred. In a closed paper bag, or in a bowl covered with a plate, steam the pepper until cool. Rub away the burned peel, stem and core the pepper, and dice the flesh.

In a medium saucepan over low heat, melt the butter. Add the onions and thyme and cook, covered, stirring once or twice, for 10 minutes. Whisk the flour into the onion mixture and cook, stirring, for 3 minutes. Whisk the stock into the flour mixture, stir in the salt and freshly ground black pepper, and bring to a simmer. Cook uncovered, stirring occasionally, until thickened to a medium gravy, 15 to 20 minutes. Stir the diced pheasant, chopped sweet red pepper, corn, and peas into the gravy. Adjust the seasoning. *The recipe can be prepared to this point several hours ahead. Reheat the pheasant mixture to simmering before proceeding with the recipe.*

Position a rack in the upper third of the oven and preheat the oven to 400°F.

Spoon the hot pheasant mixture into a deep 3-quart baking dish. Divide the corn bread batter into 8 equal portions and dollop them on top of the pheasant mixture, distributing them evenly. Bake about 35 minutes, or until the pheasant mixture is bubbling and the corn bread topping is puffed, firm, and lightly browned. Let the casserole rest 5 minutes before serving.

serves 8

chapter eight

feathered fare
chicken, turkey, and duck

We happen to think the national bird should be the chicken—panfried, preferably—and we're not alone among Texans in honoring that crisp, brown, and juicy critter above all the eagles in the land. Talk about noble! Turkey, too, we celebrate, at Thanksgiving as well as at all other times of the year, as much for its nutritional and budgetary pluses as for its good eating. (Surprised? Don't be. This is modern Texas and those rangy cowpokes standing down by the corral are probably discussing their respective cholesterol levels.) In this chapter feathered fare gets to shine. Here you will find—among other delights—a handsomely browned holiday turkey, and a thoroughly modern grilled chicken and pasta salad, as well as what what we believe to be the best fried chicken recipe on the planet—and much more.

fired chicken with pink pan gravy

The chili powder blend added to the flour that coats this fried chicken fires things up just enough (Park likes it hotter—if you do too, add 2 teaspoons freshly ground black pepper along with the chili powder). The gravy turns out slightly pink and slightly hot—it's delicious over Perfectly Lumpy Mashed Potatoes (page 184). During hot weather, we skip the gravy and serve the chicken cooled just to room temperature—it makes great picnic fare.

2 cups cultured buttermilk
1 tablespoon hot pepper sauce
2 3½- to 4-pound chickens, each
    cut into 8 serving pieces
1¾ cups unbleached all-purpose
    flour
½ cup mild chili powder blend

3 teaspoons salt
About 2 pounds solid vegetable
    shortening
4 cups milk
½ teaspoon freshly ground black
    pepper

In a bowl, whisk together the buttermilk and hot pepper sauce. Pour the buttermilk over the chicken pieces in a deep bowl, cover, and let marinate at room temperature for 2 hours, stirring once or twice.

In a pie plate, thoroughly mix together 1½ cups of the flour, the chili powder blend, and 2 teaspoons of the salt. One at a time, lift the chicken pieces from the buttermilk, letting most of the excess drip back into the bowl, and dredge the chicken in the seasoned flour. Let the floured chicken pieces rest uncovered on a rack for 30 minutes to firm the coating.

In two large deep skillets over medium heat, melt the shortening—it should be deep enough to come about halfway up the sides of the largest pieces of chicken. When the shortening is very hot, add the chicken pieces skin-side down. Cook, uncovered, for 12 minutes. Turn the chicken pieces and cook, uncovered, another 12 to 15 minutes, or until they are crisp and a deep reddish-brown. Transfer them to absorbent paper to drain.

Pour off the fat, straining it to remove the cracklings and reserving ¼ cup of it. In one of the two skillets combine the reserved fat, the cracklings, and any crisp bits that can be scraped from the other skillet. Set over low heat. Whisk in the remaining ¼ cup flour and cook, stirring often, for 5 minutes.

Slowly whisk in the milk. Stir in 1 teaspoon salt and the freshly ground black pepper and bring the gravy to a simmer. Cook uncovered, stirring often and scraping the bottom of the pan, until the gravy has thickened, about 7 minutes. Adjust the seasoning and serve over mashed potatoes, accompanying the chicken.

serves 8

pollo deshebrada
(shredded chicken)

Here is our method for cooking and shredding chicken to be used in tacos, quesadillas, flautas, burritos, and so on. Be certain to save the broth (there will be about 2 quarts) for use in soups. Though the meat will not be as moist (and there won't be a bonus of broth), if time is tight you may substitute an already roasted chicken from the supermarket. Just discard the skin, pull the meat from the bones, and shred it.

1 4½- to 5-pound young chicken, quartered, plus the giblets except the liver
2 garlic cloves, peeled and minced
1 teaspoon oregano, crumbled

1 teaspoon salt
½ teaspoon freshly ground black pepper
2 bay leaves

In a wide 5-quart pan, arrange the chicken quarters in a single layer. Add cold water to cover by 1 inch (about 2½ quarts) and set over medium heat. Stir in the giblets, garlic, oregano, salt, freshly ground black pepper, and bay leaves and bring to a simmer. Partially cover the pan and lower the heat. Simmer the chicken, turning it once at the halfway point, until the meat is tender and falling from the bone, about 25 minutes.

Remove the pan from the heat, set it on a rack, and let the chicken cool to room temperature, uncovered, in the poaching liquid. Drain the chicken and strain and degrease the broth, reserving it for another use. Skin the chicken, remove and shred the meat. Cover and refrigerate. *The chicken can be cooked up to 1 day ahead.*

makes about 4 cups

a chicken dinner in winter

Chile con Queso (page 12) with Warmed Corn Tortillas

Fired Chicken with Pink Pan Gravy (page 146)
Perfectly Lumpy Mashed Potatoes (page 184)
Calico Corn (page 182)
Masa Biscuits (page 192)

Norma's Quick and Easy Frozen Mango Dessert (page 232)
Bizcochos (page 220)

a chicken dinner in summer

Grilled Shrimp Quesadillas (page 19)

Cold Fired Chicken (page 146)
Jalapeño-Pineapple Coleslaw (page 199)
Roasted New Potato Salad with Green Chiles (page 201)

Peach Cobbler (page 210)
Mango-Peach Ice Cream with Dulce Crunch (page 230)

grilled chicken and pasta salad with margarita mayonnaise

In our continuing quest for zesty, interesting cold food to keep hungry guests happy even when the weather is hot, we found this untraditional but delicious main course salad. What began as an improvised way to stretch some leftover grilled chicken and a serendipitous box of pasta into supper for some drop-in company has evolved into a full-fledged and very colorful plate of party food, worthy of a trip to the store for its ingredients. Present this on one big platter as part of a hot-weather buffet, or for a seated lunch or supper arrange an individually garnished plate for each diner.

¼ cup olive oil
¼ cup fresh orange juice
2 tablespoons mild chili powder
    blend
1 tablespoon hot pepper sauce
2¼ teaspoons salt
2¼ pounds boneless, skinless
    chicken breasts, trimmed of fat
    and connective tissue
2 cups mesquite wood smoking
    chips
1 pound imported short semolina
    pasta, such as penne rigate or
    fusilli

Margarita Mayonnaise (page 150)
¾ cup diced red onion
2 heads of romaine, separated into
    leaves, rinsed, and patted dry
3 medium ripe tomatoes, trimmed
    and cut into wedges
2 buttery-ripe black-skinned
    avocados, pitted and cut into thin
    unpeeled wedges

In a medium bowl, whisk together the olive oil, orange juice, chili powder blend, hot pepper sauce, and ¼ teaspoon of the salt. Add the chicken breasts, turn them to coat, and marinate them at room temperature, covered, turning them once or twice more, for 1 hour.

Soak the wood chips in water for at least 30 minutes.

Preheat a gas grill (medium-high) or light a charcoal fire and let it burn down until the coals are evenly white. Drain the wood chips and scatter them over the firestones or coals. Position the rack about 6 inches above the heat source and cover the grill. When the wood chips are smoking, lay the chicken breasts on the grill rack and cook, covered, turning them once or twice and basting them with the remaining marinade, until they are just cooked through, about 4 minutes per side. Transfer them to a plate and cool to room temperature.

Bring a large pot of water to a rolling boil. Stir in the remaining 2 teaspoons of salt and the pasta and cook, stirring occasionally, until the pasta is just tender, about 9 minutes. Drain it well, rinse it under cold water, and drain again.

Tear the chicken into bite-size pieces. In a large bowl, toss together the chicken, pasta, and mayonnaise. Add the red onions and toss again. Adjust the seasoning.

Line a platter or individual plates with the romaine. Mound the chicken salad on top of the romaine and garnish with the tomato and avocado wedges.

serves 6 to 8

margarita mayonnaise

This mayonnaise is also good as a sauce for poached or grilled seafood, and it makes a wonderful dip for raw vegetables.

3 egg yolks	1 tablespoon gold tequila
¼ cup fresh orange juice	1½ teaspoons salt
Minced zest (colored peel) of 2 large oranges	1 teaspoon dry mustard
	½ teaspoon freshly ground black pepper
3 tablespoons Grand Marnier	
2 tablespoons fresh lime juice	2½ cups corn oil

In a food processor, combine the egg yolks, orange juice, orange zest, Grand Marnier, lime juice, tequila, salt, dry mustard, and freshly ground black pepper. Process until smooth. With the motor running, add the corn oil through the feed tube in a quick, steady stream. The mayonnaise will thicken. Adjust the seasoning and process to blend. Transfer to a storage container, cover, and refrigerate. *The mayonnaise can be prepared up to 3 days ahead.*

makes about 3 cups

a cold summer patio supper for a crowd

A Big Galvanized Tub Full of Well-Iced Texas and New Mexico White Wines

Pico de Gallo (page 3) and Corn, Black Bean, and Roasted Red Pepper Salsa (page 7) and Santos's Salsa Verde (page 6) and Guacamole (page 10) with Tostaditas (page 32)

El Paso Gazpacho with Garlic-Shrimp Salad (page 96)
Salpicón (page 120) with Warmed Corn Tortillas
Grilled Chicken and Pasta Salad with Margarita Mayonnaise (page 149)

Long-stemmed Strawberries Dipped into Warm Cajeta
Iced Kahlúa Coffee (page 243)

small chickens marinated in tequila and lime

If a couple of margaritas make *you* feel tender, imagine what the same ingredients will do for these little birds! The marinade here moves our favorite Southwestern cocktail from the bar to the table by way of the kitchen and results in moist and savory chickens every time. Cook them completely through in the oven, or remove them 10 minutes early and finish them on a preheated grill over smoking wood chips for extra flavor. Sometimes we send away to Balducci's in New York for a batch of the teenage chickens called poussins, but, honestly, game hens from the supermarket work just fine.

4 Cornish hens, preferably fresh or
  poussins (about 1¼ pounds each)
½ cup fresh lime juice
⅓ cup gold tequila
¼ cup olive oil

2 tablespoons Triple Sec or other
  orange liqueur
2 garlic cloves, peeled and minced
½ teaspoon salt
¼ teaspoon freshly ground black
  pepper

With poultry shears or a long sharp knife, cut away the backbone from each chicken. With the palm of your hand, flatten the birds, cracking the breastbones as you do so. In a large bowl, combine the lime juice, tequila, olive oil, Triple Sec, and garlic. Add the chickens and turn them to coat with the marinade. Cover them and let them stand at room temperature, turning them once or twice more, for 2 hours.

Position a rack in the upper third of the oven and preheat the oven to 400°F.

Remove the chickens from the marinade and arrange them skin-side up on a jelly roll pan. Season them with the salt and freshly ground black pepper. Bake the chickens, basting them occasionally with the marinade, until the skin is golden and the juices from the thighs, pricked at their thickest, run pinkish-yellow, 25 to 30 minutes. Serve them hot, warm, or cool.

serves 4

a little dinner party

Chorizo Quesadillas (page 19)
Santos's Salsa Verde (page 6)

Small Chickens Marinated in Tequila and Lime (page 152)
Calico Corn (page 182)
Perfectly Lumpy Mashed Potatoes (page 184)

Mode à la Pecan Pie (page 216)

spanish mission chicken

Sherry, olives, raisins, and almonds, plus a generous helping of garlic, flavor this colorful chicken dish inspired by El Paso's long history as a center of Spanish missionary work. Two missions, at Ysleta and Socorro, dating originally to the fifteenth century, as well as the chapel at the sixteenth-century Presidio San Elizario, are still standing today. Linked by the Historic Mission Trail, they serve as beautiful daily reminders of El Paso's link with the past and with Spain.

¼ cup slivered almonds
1¾ cups chicken broth, homemade or canned
½ cup dark raisins
2 3½-pound chickens, quartered
12 large whole garlic cloves, peeled
2 tablespoons olive oil
½ teaspoon salt
¼ teaspoon freshly ground black pepper

¾ cup medium-dry (Amontillado) sherry
3 tablespoons unsalted butter, softened
3 tablespoons unbleached all-purpose flour
24 unpitted small green olives, drained

Preheat the oven to 375°F.

Spread the slivered almonds in a shallow metal pan (like a cake tin) and toast them, stirring occasionally, until crisp and golden, about 8 minutes. Transfer them to a bowl and cool. In a small saucepan, bring the chicken broth to a simmer. Stir in the raisins, remove from the heat, and cool to room temperature. Strain, reserving the raisins and broth separately.

Position a rack in the upper third of the oven and turn the oven down to 350°F.

Pat the chicken quarters dry. Arrange them in a shallow baking dish just large enough to accommodate them in a single layer. Scatter the garlic cloves over the chicken quarters. Drizzle the chicken and garlic with the olive oil. Sprinkle the chicken and garlic with the salt and freshly ground black pepper.

Bake for 15 minutes. Baste with half the sherry and bake for another 15 minutes. Baste with the remaining sherry and bake another 30 to 40 minutes, basting every 10 minutes with the accumulated pan juices, or until the chicken is golden and juices from a thigh, when pricked at its thickest, run clear yellow. Transfer the chicken quarters to a heated platter and tent them with foil.

Strain and degrease the pan juices, reserving the garlic cloves. Force the garlic through a sieve into a medium saucepan. Stir in the degreased pan juices and the raisin-soaking broth and set over medium heat. Bring to a simmer and cook uncovered, stirring and skimming, for 10 minutes. In a small bowl, mash the butter and flour together into a paste. Turn the heat to low and gradually whisk the flour paste into the broth mixture. Stir in the raisins and olives and simmer until the sauce is thick, 3 to 4 minutes. Adjust the seasoning. Spoon some of the sauce over the chicken, scatter the almonds over all, and serve immediately, passing the remaining sauce at the table.

serves 8

a mission trail menu

Dry Sherry

Thin-Sliced Smoked Ham or Prosciutto
Crusty Bread and Sweet Butter

El Paso Gazpacho with Garlic-Shrimp Salad (page 96)

Spanish Mission Chicken (page 154)
Calabacitas con Crema (page 185)
Texmati Pilaf (page 181)

Forti's Almond Flan (page 234)

---

the first thanksgiving

The feast day America observes in November as a re-creation of the Pilgrims' celebration of their good fortune in the New World is probably not in any danger of repeal. Still, it is worth noting that there is considerable historical evidence that another group of colonists celebrated their arrival in North America with a feast of thanksgiving some twenty-three years ahead of the colonists on the East Coast, near what was to become El Paso. On April 30, 1598, it was recorded that those on Don Juan de Oñate's colonizing expedition, recovering from their long, dry journey north to Santa Fe from Santa Barbara, Mexico, paused en route at the pass of the north to lay claim to the land for the king of Spain and then sealed their joy with a great repast of, among other things, "roasted meat and fish." In El Paso this has given us another day of the year on which to eat well and to stage a costumed drama, a favorite and frequent El Paso event. There has been idle talk around town of ignoring the November feast. At the Kerr households, however, we have no intention of trading in one holiday for another, not when two can be celebrated with historical impunity and good food—a state of affairs truly worth giving thanks for.

roast turkey with browned garlic gravy

The turkey is native to North America, and in the Southwest it has been prized eating for centuries. Today, in modern El Paso, turkey is one of the great staples, and ground turkey, turkey cold cuts, and so on crowd the supermarket cases as they do elsewhere. On Thanksgiving, too, turkey is essential fare, and while an authentic batch of the rich and complex Mexican national dish *mole poblano de guajolote* would not be out of place, we prefer a traditional roast turkey, albeit in a menu with a few Southwestern touches. Fresh turkeys, without that nasty yellow self-basting stuff injected into them, are better eating. This recipe makes enough gravy to serve as either a sauce for the turkey or over mashed potatoes (if you are serving them) but not both.

TURKEY
1 12-pound turkey, preferably fresh, including the neck and giblets except the liver
1½ cups chopped onion
3 large carrots, peeled and chopped
12 unpeeled whole garlic cloves
¼ cup olive oil
Salt to taste
Freshly ground black pepper to taste
½ cup chicken broth, homemade or canned
½ cup dry white wine

GRAVY
¾ stick (6 tablespoons) unsalted butter
6 tablespoons unbleached all-purpose flour
Degreased juices from the turkey roasting pan
About 5 cups chicken broth, homemade or canned
Salt to taste
Freshly ground black pepper to taste

continued

FOR THE TURKEY

Position a rack in the lower third of the oven and preheat the oven to 325°F.

Rinse the turkey inside and out and pat it dry. Pull any visible fat from the cavity and cut off and reserve the first joint of each wing. Set the turkey in a roasting pan. Scatter the onions, carrots, garlic, turkey neck, giblets, and reserved wing tips around the turkey. Rub 1 tablespoon of the olive oil into the skin of the turkey breast. Season generously with salt and freshly ground black pepper. Dampen a 10- by 20-inch piece of cheesecloth. Double the cheesecloth and drape it over the turkey breast. In a bowl, mix together the remaining olive oil, chicken broth, and wine.

Set the turkey in the oven and roast it for 30 minutes. Baste the turkey through the cheesecloth with half the wine mixture and roast it another 30 minutes. Baste the turkey again with the remaining wine mixture and roast it another 15 minutes. Baste the turkey with the accumulated pan juices and continue to roast, basting it every 15 minutes, for a total cooking time of about 2¾ hours. The turkey is done when an instant-reading thermometer inserted into the thickest part of the thigh registers 170°F and the drumsticks move easily in their joints. Transfer the turkey to a cutting board and tent it with foil.

Scrape any browned bits from the bottom of the roasting pan and pour the solids and roasting juices into a strainer set over a bowl. Press hard with the back of the spoon to extract as much juice as possible. Discard the solids; degrease the pan juices.

FOR THE GRAVY

In a medium saucepan over low heat, melt the butter. When it foams, whisk in the flour and cook, stirring often without allowing the flour to brown, for 5 minutes. Combine the pan juices with enough of the chicken broth to equal 6 cups. Whisk the broth mixture into the flour and butter. Bring the gravy to a simmer and cook, partially covered, stirring occasionally, for about 20 minutes, or until the gravy has thickened slightly. Season with salt and freshly ground black pepper to taste. Carve the turkey and serve it accompanied by the gravy.

serves 12

a southwestern thanksgiving feast

Moyer Champagne Texas Brut Especial NV

Texas Trash (page 17)

Mesquite-Smoked Shrimp-in-the-Shell (page 81) and
Lettuce with Avocado-Buttermilk Salad Dressing (page 203)

Cream of Green Chile Soup (page 101)

Llano Estacado Texas Cabernet Sauvignon

Roast Turkey with Browned Garlic Gravy (page 157)
Corn Bread, Apple, and Pine Nut Dressing with Fresh Sage (page 188)
Mashed Sweet Potatoes (page 184)
Edythe May's Mango Salad (page 198)
Calico Corn (page 182)
Jalapeño-Cranberry Relish (page 204)
Masa Biscuits (page 192)

Crepes with Cajeta and Pecans (page 226)

mole verde con pato
(braised duck in a green pumpkin seed sauce)

The classic dark brown mole of Pueblo (the one with the chocolate) is not the only complex sauce that goes by that name. Green mole is another great dish of Mexico, and the excellent commercially prepared version used in this recipe lets the cook turn out this wonderfully dramatic-looking and tasty dish with the minimum of fuss. There is a generous amount of the verdant sauce—either plain white rice or Perfectly Lumpy Mashed Potatoes (page 184) will serve as its necessary absorbent partner. Chicken can be substituted for the duck (shorten the oven time to about 30 minutes), but duck and this richly flavored sauce are a much more delicious combination. Pumpkin seeds can be found in health food stores.

¼ cup pumpkin seeds
2 4½- to 5-pound domestic
    ducklings, including giblets
    except the livers
¼ cup olive oil
1 cup chopped onion

1 medium carrot, peeled and
    chopped
2¼ cups chicken broth, homemade
    or canned
1 8¼-ounce jar commercial mole
    verde paste
Salt to taste

Position a rack in the upper third of the oven and preheat the oven to 375°F.

In a single layer in a metal baking dish (like a cake tin), roast the pumpkin seeds until they have puffed and are crisp and lightly browned, about 8 minutes. Cool and then coarsely chop them.

Pull all visible fat from the ducks. Cut away and reserve the necks and the first wing segments. With a long sharp knife or poultry shears, cut away the backbones and quarter the ducks. Trim away any excess skin and pat the duck quarters dry. Prick the skin of the duck quarters lightly with the tines of a fork.

In a heavy flameproof casserole with a tight-fitting lid (it should be just large enough to accommodate the duck quarters in a single layer), warm 2 tablespoons of the olive oil over medium heat. Working in batches, cook the duck quarters, turning them once or twice, until they are very brown, 15 to 20 minutes. (The skin side, especially, should be as brown and crisp as possible.) Transfer the browned duck quarters to a plate. Pour off and discard the fat but do not clean the casserole.

Position a rack in the middle of the oven and turn the oven down to 350°F.

In the casserole over medium-high heat, warm the remaining olive oil. Pat the giblets, wing tips, and necks dry and cook them, turning occasionally, until lightly browned, about 7 minutes. Stir in the onions and carrots and cook, covered, stirring once or twice and scraping the browned deposits from the bottom of the pan, for 10 minutes. Arrange the duck quarters over the giblets and vegetables, pour the chicken broth over everything, and cover the casserole. Bake about 50 minutes, or until the duck meat is tender.

Transfer the duck quarters to a warmed platter and tent it with foil. Strain and degrease the braising juices. Transfer them to a medium saucepan and set over low heat. Whisk the mole verde paste into the sauce. When the sauce is smooth and heated through, taste it and adjust the seasoning, adding salt to taste. Arrange the duck quarters on plates and nap with the sauce. Sprinkle the sauce with the chopped pumpkin seeds and serve immediately.

serves 4

an elegant dinner party

La Buena Vida Texas Springtown Mist (Blanc de Noir)

Clear Chicken Broth with Shrimp, Corn, and Cilantro (page 99)

Ste. Genevieve Texas Fumé Blanc Grand Reserve

Mole Verde con Pato (page 160)
White Rice
Calabacitas con Crema (page 185)

Crepes with Cajeta and Pecans (page 226)

chapter nine

rise and shine!
breakfast and brunch

Like the rest of the country, Texas doesn't spend as much time chowing down in the morning as it used to. ☀ There's just so little time and we're watching our weight and who'll do the dishes and so on and so on. ☀ We miss those days of groaning breakfast tables of assorted edibles, none of them selected for their high fiber or their low fat content. ☀ Like plates of steaks or incendiary bowls of chili, the Southwestern breakfast is part Texas myth (but it's based on the truth) and it's the kind of myth that, from time to time, we endeavor to re-create. ☀ Middle-of-the-week breakfasts may still be yogurt and granola, but Saturday and Sunday are definitely reserved for the kind of hearty, ranch house dining we dream about the other five days of the week.

huevos rancheros
(fried eggs with ranch-style tomato-chile sauce)

This zesty breakfast classic is so widely popular in El Paso it's practically diner fare, and for many locals the sauce can't be too hot. We've modulated things just slightly, mornings being a fairly tender time for many folks, but you can always fire it up or down as you wish. The dish, always one of our favorite restaurant meals, has lately become a favorite at home as well, one we serve often for a casual brunch. Speaking of diners, if you haven't worked in one and don't feel like coping with six orders of sunny-side up eggs, try scrambling them instead. The results look unconventional but taste just fine. Of the two accompaniments (we think they're essential to the success of the dish), the frijoles refritos can be prepared a day ahead and reheated, but the Texmati pilaf should be freshly made.

RANCHERO SAUCE
5 long green chiles
3 large ripe tomatoes (about 1½ pounds total), stemmed, cored, and chunked
1 cup chopped onion
¼ cup chicken broth, homemade or canned
2 garlic cloves, peeled and minced
1 fresh jalapeño chile, stemmed and minced
1 teaspoon salt
½ teaspoon dried oregano, crumbled
2 tablespoons olive oil

EGGS
About 1½ cups corn oil
12 6-inch corn tortillas
¾ stick (6 tablespoons) unsalted butter
12 eggs

TO ASSEMBLE
1 recipe Frijoles Refritos (page 179), heated until steaming
1 recipe Texmati Pilaf (page 181)
½ cup grated feta cheese, for garnish for the frijoles refritos (optional)

FOR THE SAUCE
In the open flame of a gas burner or under a preheated broiler, roast the long green chiles, turning them, until they are lightly but evenly charred. Steam the chiles in a paper bag, or in a bowl, covered with a plate, until cool. Rub away the burned peel. Stem and seed the chiles and coarsely chop them. There should be about ¾ cup.

In a blender, combine the tomatoes, onions, chicken broth, garlic, jalapeño, salt, and oregano and blend until smooth. In a medium saucepan over moderate heat, warm the olive oil. When it is hot, add the purée (it may spatter) and stir in the chopped green chiles. Bring to a simmer and cook, partially covered, stirring once or twice, for 15 minutes. Adjust the seasoning. *The sauce can be prepared 1 day ahead. Cool, cover, and refrigerate. Warm over low heat, stirring often, before using.*

FOR THE EGGS
In a deep skillet, warm about ½ inch of corn oil over medium heat. Using tongs, dip the tortillas one at a time into the oil, turn them, and then transfer them to absorbent paper and keep them warm. The tortillas should be in the oil no more than a few seconds, and it should not be hot enough to crisp them.

In each of two large skillets melt half the butter. Crack the eggs 2 at a time into a small bowl. Slide each pair of eggs into the hot butter and cook them until the whites are firm but the yolks remain somewhat soft.

TO ASSEMBLE
Arrange 2 warm tortillas, overlapping slightly, on each of 6 warmed plates. Place a pair of eggs on each pair of tortillas. Spoon a large dollop of frijoles refritos onto one side of each plate and a large spoonful of Texmati pilaf onto the other side. Spoon the ranchero sauce evenly over the eggs, using it all. Sprinkle the frijoles with the feta cheese, if you are using it, and serve immediately.

serves 6

masa biscuits with ham and green chile gravy

Biscuits and gravy are hearty, no-nonsense food but they generate more than a little breakfast excitement when that gravy is studded with nubbins of good ham and chopped roasted green chiles. Serve the biscuits alongside fried or scrambled eggs and drink chilled fresh orange or grapefruit juice.

5 long green chiles	¼ cup unbleached all-purpose flour
¾ stick (6 tablespoons) unsalted butter	5 cups milk
	½ teaspoon salt
1 pound firm, smoky ham, trimmed and cut into ¼-inch cubes	8 freshly baked Masa Biscuits (page 192), split

In the open flame of a gas burner or under a preheated broiler, roast the long green chiles, turning them, until they are lightly but evenly charred. Steam the chiles in a paper bag, or in a bowl, covered with a plate, until cool. Rub away the burned peel. Stem and seed the chiles and coarsely chop them. There should be about ¾ cup.

In a large skillet over medium-low heat, melt the butter. Add the ham cubes and cook them, stirring occasionally, until lightly browned, about 10 minutes. Sprinkle the flour over the ham cubes and cook, stirring constantly, for 5 minutes. Slowly whisk the milk into the ham mixture. Stir in the green chiles and salt. Raise the heat to medium and bring the milk mixture to a simmer. Cook, stirring occasionally and scraping the bottom of the pan, until thickened into a medium gravy, about 7 minutes. Adjust the seasoning.

Arrange the biscuits, split-sides up, on 8 plates. Spoon the gravy over and around them, using it all. Serve immediately.

serves 8

a hearty brunch

Classic Tequila Sunrises (page 238)

Chile con Queso (page 12) with
Tostaditas (page 32)

Masa Biscuits with Ham and Green Chile Gravy (page 166)
Scrambled Eggs

Chilled Fresh Citrus Sections

burrito desayuno
(breakfast burrito with eggs, cheese, potatoes, and chorizo)

This sturdy workingman's breakfast has acquired a kind of chic, thanks in part to its popularity up north in trendy Santa Fe and in part to how good it tastes. It's popular in El Paso too, of course, and wherever else people like to start off the day well fed and fired up. If you would like to go meatless the chorizo is optional, but the Pico de Gallo and the Frijoles Refritos (black or pinto) are, to the Kerrs at least, essential. If it's really breakfast you're preparing, serve strong coffee or Whipped Mexican Chocolate (page 242); at brunch enjoy a cold beer or a tall Classic Tequila Sunrise (page 238). Please note that the filling, minus the cheese and tortillas, can be enjoyed on its own, as glorified scrambled eggs.

4 long green chiles
5 medium boiling potatoes (about 2½ pounds), peeled and cut into ½-inch cubes
2¾ teaspoons salt
5 tablespoons unsalted butter
1¼ cups coarsely chopped onion
½ pound chorizo, cooked and crumbled

10 eggs
3 cups (about 12 ounces) grated cheese, preferably a combination of Monterey Jack cheese and medium-sharp cheddar cheese
8 10-inch flour tortillas
Frijoles Refritos (page 179)
Pico de Gallo (page 3)

In the open flame of a gas burner or under a preheated broiler, roast the long green chiles, turning them, until they are lightly but evenly charred. Steam the chiles in a paper bag, or in a bowl, covered with a plate, until cool. Rub away the burned peel. Stem and seed the chiles and coarsely chop them. There should be about ½ cup.

In a medium saucepan, cover the diced potatoes with cold water. Stir in 2 teaspoons of the salt, set over medium heat, and bring to a boil. Cook, stirring once or twice, until just tender, about 5 minutes. Drain. *The chiles and potatoes can be prepared up to 1 day ahead. Wrap them well and refrigerate.*

In a large skillet, preferably nonstick, over medium heat, melt the butter. Stir in the onions and potatoes and cook, stirring occasionally, until lightly browned, about 10 minutes. Stir in the chorizo and chopped green chiles and cook another 3 minutes. In a large bowl, whisk the eggs with ¾ teaspoon salt. Stir the eggs into the potato mixture and cook until just set, 3 to 4 minutes. Fold in the cheese, remove the skillet from the heat, and let stand, covered, for 3 to 4 minutes, or until the cheese is melted.

Warm the flour tortillas slightly. Spoon ⅛ of the egg mixture into the center of a tortilla. Fold in the sides and roll the tortilla to enclose the filling. Repeat this with the rest of the filling and tortillas. Arrange the burritos on warmed plates and serve immediately, accompanied by frijoles refritos and pico de gallo.

serves 8

an easy brunch

Three-Alarm Bloody Marys (page 240)

Burritos Desayuno (page 168)
Pico de Gallo (page 3)

Grilled Pineapple with Cajeta (page 228)

---

whole wheat and toasted pecan flapjacks

These Texas-scale flapjacks are grainy, nutty, and irresistible, whether topped with warmed maple syrup, honey, cinnamon-sugar, or homemade jam. Serve them with panfried ham steaks or good, smoky bacon, and remember that for a quicker A.M. start the pecans can be toasted and the dry ingredients combined the night before.

4 cups (about 14 ounces) pecans
1½ cups unbleached all-purpose
  flour
1½ cups whole wheat flour, preferably stone-ground
2 teaspoons baking powder
1½ teaspoons salt
4 eggs
⅓ cup packed light brown sugar

3¼ cups cultured buttermilk, at
  room temperature
1½ sticks (6 ounces) unsalted
  butter, melted, plus additional
  butter for the griddle, and, if
  desired, for topping the finished
  pancakes
Maple syrup, cinnamon-sugar,
  honey, or jam, as topping

Position a rack in the middle of the oven and preheat to 375°F. Spread the pecans in a metal baking pan that will hold them in a single layer and bake, stirring once or twice, until the pecans are crisp, brown, and fragrant, about 10 minutes. Remove them from the pan, cool to room temperature, and coarsely chop them.

In a large mixing bowl, stir together the white and whole wheat flours, baking powder, and salt. In a medium bowl, whisk the eggs. Whisk in the brown sugar and then the buttermilk. Add the buttermilk mixture and the 1½ sticks melted butter alternately to the dry ingredients. When almost combined, stir in the pecans. Do not overmix.

Over medium heat, warm a pancake griddle. Brush it with butter. Working in batches, drop the batter onto the griddle by heaping half cupfuls. Flatten the batter into 6-inch rounds. Fry for about 4 minutes, or until steam holes appear on the tops of the pancakes. Turn them and fry another 2 to 3 minutes, or until fully cooked through and lightly browned. Repeat with the remaining batter, buttering the griddle between batches as necessary. Serve immediately, accompanied by additional butter, maple syrup, cinnamon-sugar, honey, or jam.

16 large pancakes, serving 8 or more

bacon–blue cornmeal waffles with jalapeño jelly syrup

Greater dedication hath no morning cook than to stand at the waffle iron, turning out these crisp treats to order—which is really the best way to enjoy them. The bacon cooks right into the waffles as they cook which makes for an eye-catching presentation. The buttery, sweet-hot syrup, adapted from a recipe by *The Silver Palate Cookbook* researcher and veteran arts publicist Amy Campbell Lamphere, is an unexpected (and only slightly *picante*) morning eye-opener. Be sure to use thin-sliced bacon or it won't be cooked by the time the waffles are done.

1 cup unbleached all-purpose flour
¾ cup blue cornmeal, preferably stone-ground
1 tablespoon sugar
2 teaspoons baking powder
¼ teaspoon salt
3 eggs, separated

1½ cups milk
6 tablespoons unsalted butter, melted
9 strips thin bacon, halved cross-wise
Jalapeño Jelly Syrup (page 172), warmed

Preheat a waffle iron according to the manufacturer's directions. Sift the flour, cornmeal, sugar, baking powder, and salt into a large bowl. In a small bowl, whisk the eggs yolks. Whisk in the milk and melted butter. In a medium bowl, whisk the egg whites until stiff peaks form. Stir the milk mixture into the dry ingredients, mixing only until just combined. Fold in the egg whites; do not overmix.

If the waffle iron is well seasoned, there is no need to grease it. Spoon between ½ and ⅔ cup of the batter onto the waffle iron (the grid should be about ¾ full). Lay 3 pieces of bacon side by side across the batter. Close the waffle iron and cook 4 to 5 minutes, or until the waffle is golden brown and the bacon is cooked until just crisp. (If using a waffle iron that sits on a stove burner, cook the waffle, bacon-side down, for 3½ minutes, turn, and cook another 2 minutes.)

Transfer the waffle to a plate and serve immediately, accompanied by jalapeño jelly syrup. Repeat with the remaining batter, bacon, and syrup.

serves 6

jalapeño jelly syrup

Select a jalapeño jelly that is hot, not too sweet, with plenty of honest jalapeño flavor. (One way to be certain of these three conditions is to look for The El Paso Chile Company label!) The syrup takes only minutes to prepare, but it can be done ahead if you wish. Leftovers keep well for use at another meal.

1½ cups jalapeño pepper jelly   ¼ cup honey
6 tablespoons unsalted butter

In a small saucepan over low heat, combine the jelly, butter, and honey. Cook, stirring, until the butter is melted and the syrup is hot, about 4 minutes. *The jelly can be prepared up to 1 week ahead and refrigerated, covered. Warm over low heat before using.*

makes about 2 cups

a hunt breakfast

Strong Black Coffee with a Splash of Bourbon

Quail with Bacon (page 137)
Grits with Chiles and Cheese (page 173)
Scrambled Eggs
Pistachio Sticky Buns Baked in a Skillet (page 174)

---

grits with chiles and cheese

We have seen versions of this easy casserole calling for up to a pound of cheese for a mere six diners. That is rich and delicious eating, all right, but extravagant for a side dish, which is how we prefer this versatile recipe. It usually shows up at breakfast in our house accompanying eggs, bacon, ham steaks, or panfried quail, but it's also useful at lunch or supper. If you want it spicier, sauté a chopped fresh jalapeño along with the onion and garlic.

6 long green chiles
½ stick (4 tablespoons) unsalted butter
1 cup finely chopped onion
1 clove garlic, peeled and minced
4 cups chicken broth, homemade or canned
1 cup regular-cooking ("old-fashioned") hominy grits

½ teaspoon salt
½ teaspoon freshly ground black pepper
3 eggs
2 cups (about 8 ounces) grated Monterey Jack cheese or medium-sharp cheddar cheese or a combination of both

In the open flame of a gas burner or under a preheated broiler, roast the long green chiles, turning them, until they are lightly but evenly charred. Steam the chiles in a paper bag, or in a bowl, covered with a plate, until cool. Rub away the burned peel. Stem and seed the chiles and coarsely chop them. There should be about 1 cup.

Position a rack in the middle of the oven and preheat the oven to 350°F.

Butter a 2-quart casserole.

In a heavy 5-quart pan over low heat, melt the butter. Add the onions and garlic and cook, covered, stirring once or twice, for 10 minutes. Stir in the chicken broth and bring to a boil. Stir in the grits, salt, and freshly ground black pepper and return the mixture to the boil. Lower the heat, loosely cover (the grits mixture will splatter as it thickens), and cook, stirring often, for 20 minutes.

In a medium bowl, whisk the eggs. Whisk 1 cup of the hot grits into the eggs, then whisk this egg and grits mixture back into the pan of grits. Stir in the grated cheese and chiles and adjust the seasoning. Spoon the grits mixture into the buttered casserole and bake about 40 minutes, or until it is puffed and lightly browned and evenly but not firmly set. Let stand 5 minutes on a rack before serving.

serves 6 to 8

pistachio sticky buns baked in a skillet

These high, wide, and handsome sweet rolls don't have to be baked in a skillet (you can substitute a 13- by 9- by 2-inch baking dish if you wish), but when they are it recalls—especially if they're where your guests can see them cooling in the skillet—rustic chuck wagon sweets of yore and makes for an eye-catching presentation.

DOUGH
2 cups milk
1 stick (4 ounces) unsalted butter
3 tablespoons sugar
3 teaspoons salt
1 package dry yeast
½ teaspoon ground cinnamon
3 well-beaten eggs, at room
    temperature
About 7 cups unbleached all-
    purpose flour

TO ASSEMBLE
1¾ sticks (7 ounces) unsalted
    butter, softened
¾ cup golden raisins
1 cup shelled pistachios, from about
    ½ pound
⅔ cup light brown sugar
½ cup honey

FOR THE DOUGH

In a saucepan over medium heat, combine the milk, butter, sugar, and salt. Heat, stirring once or twice, until the butter is melted. Remove from the heat and pour into a large mixing bowl.

Cool the milk to between 105°F and 115°F. Add the yeast and cinnamon, stirring to combine, and let stand 5 minutes. Stir in the beaten eggs and then the flour, 1 cup at a time, until a soft dough forms. Turn out onto a floured surface and knead, incorporating more flour as necessary, until the dough is smooth and elastic, about 5 minutes. Butter a large bowl and turn the dough in the butter to coat it. Cover with a clean towel and let stand at room temperature for 2 hours, or until doubled in bulk. Punch down the dough, knead it briefly, and return it to the bowl. Cover with plastic wrap and refrigerate overnight.

TO ASSEMBLE

Turn the chilled dough out onto a lightly floured surface and pat and roll it out into a 12- by 17-inch rectangle about ⅓ inch thick. Spread ¾ stick of the softened butter evenly over the dough. Scatter the raisins evenly over the butter. Starting with the long side of the dough closest to you, roll the dough up into a long cylinder. Cut the cylinder crosswise into 12 equal slices.

In a heavy 14-inch skillet, preferably one with straight sides, melt the remaining 1 stick of butter. Remove from the heat and with a pastry brush grease the sides of the skillet with some of the melted butter. Stir the pistachios, light brown sugar, and honey into the butter in the skillet. Arrange the 12 slices of dough, cut-side down, in the pistachio mixture. Cover the skillet with a towel and let them rise at room temperature for 2 hours, or until doubled in bulk.

Position a rack in the middle of the oven and preheat the oven to 350°F. Set the skillet on the rack and bake 30 to 35 minutes, or until the buns are puffed and golden brown. Cool them in the skillet on a rack for 5 minutes, and then invert them onto a platter or cookie sheet. Serve hot or warm.

makes 12

chapter ten

sidekicks
beans, vegetables, quick breads,
and other accompaniments

The need for a little something on the side can't be denied. In west Texas especially, a pile of beans or rice, a big pan of corn bread or biscuits, or a mountain of mashed potatoes or savory dressing is the final touch that completes a simple menu. It may well be that we don't eat as much broccoli (or radicchio for that matter) as we should, but then zucchini and corn are durable, adaptable vegetables that we have learned from Mexico make great eating (and add color to the plate) and we rely on them and use them often.

frijoles de olla
(pot beans)

These slow-simmered beans, seasoned with a bit of bacon and red pod chiles, are delicious on their own, as well as providing the basis for a batch of well-fried beans (page 179). It's impossible to describe how good these smell simmering on the stove, and while they take some time to cook, there's little work or active supervision involved. Sorting and simmering dried beans is the kind of simple kitchen process that relaxes us after a hard day, and knowing there's a pot of beans in the refrigerator (they're good the day they're made but better the next day) is a real comfort, especially to Park's wife, Martina, who can happily make a meal of nothing more than pot beans, Pico de Gallo, and warm tortillas. For slow simmering without excessive evaporation, select a pot that is tall rather than wide. The beans are not soaked, but they should be meticulously picked over and well rinsed.

2 pounds dried pinto beans, picked over
About 3 quarts water
¼ pound sliced bacon, chopped
1 medium onion, coarsely chopped

2 or 3 dried red chile pods, rinsed, stemmed, seeded, and chopped
3 garlic cloves, peeled and chopped
4 teaspoons salt

In a large bowl, cover the beans with cold water and let stand 5 minutes. Stir thoroughly and pour through a strainer. Rinse well under cold running water. Repeat this twice.

In a tall 6- to 8-quart stockpot, combine the beans with enough cold water to cover by about 4 inches. Stir in the bacon, onions, chile pods, and garlic and set over medium heat. Bring just to a boil, then lower the heat, partially cover the pan, and simmer, stirring occasionally, for 2 hours. Stir in the salt and continue to simmer until the beans are very tender and the cooking liquid is thick, about 1 hour more. (The age of the beans, the altitude of your city, and the shape of the pot will all affect the cooking time.)

Adjust the seasoning. Serve the beans immediately or cool them to room temperature and cover. *The beans can be refrigerated for up to 3 days.*

For *Frijoles Negros de Olla* use black beans instead of pinto beans. Replace the bacon with a smoked ham hock. Thirty minutes from the time you estimate the beans will be done, stir in 4 roughly chopped sprigs—about 4 tablespoons—of epazote (page 255), if it's available. The black beans may take slightly less time than the pinto beans to become tender.

serves 12

frijoles refritos
(well-fried beans)

These are what most people call "refried beans," probably wondering all the while why they're called that, since the beans are in fact fried only once. Diana Kennedy, in her indispensable book *The Cuisines of Mexico,* has clarified the etymology, pointing out that the Mexican prefix *re* qualifies and emphasizes the word to which it is attached. Thus in the case of these beans, *refrito* means *"well*-fried," and as you'll see from this recipe, they surely are. Canned "refried" pinto beans are convenient and we resort to them on occasion (though usually as an ingredient, not for eating on their own).

2 tablespoons olive oil

6 cups Frijoles de Olla (page 178) or Frijoles Negros de Olla (above), with their liquid

In a large nonstick skillet over medium heat, warm the olive oil. Add 1 cup of the beans and, using a potato masher, crush them to a rough purée. Cook them, stirring them often with a wooden spoon, until thick, about 5 minutes. Repeat this with the rest of the frijoles, always adding them 1 cup at a time, mashing them, and then simmering them until thick before adding the next cup. The beans are done when the purée is thick and creamy—unless you like drier refritos, in which case you should fry them another 5 minutes or so, stirring constantly. *The beans can be cooked in advance and refrigerated for up to 2 days. Thin them with a bit of water and reheat them in a microwave oven or in a heavy pan over low heat, stirring often.*

serves 6

hoppin' juan

This versatile starch side dish is Norma's version of the rice-and-black-eyed-pea classic of the Old South. Touches of cumin and chile are perfectly compatible, and the results are a nice change from pot beans or well-fried beans. To make this into an easy salad, stir in 2 or 3 tablespoons of red wine vinegar and cool to room temperature. Sprinkle the salad with minced cilantro to taste, if desired, just before serving.

6 long green chiles
1½ cups dried black-eyed peas,
   picked over and rinsed
1 teaspoon salt
¼ cup olive oil

3 green onions, trimmed and sliced
   (about ½ cup)
1 garlic clove, peeled and minced
1 teaspoon ground cumin
¾ cup cooked white rice

In the open flame of a gas burner or under a preheated broiler, roast the long green chiles, turning them, until they are lightly but evenly charred. Steam the chiles in a paper bag, or in a bowl, covered with a plate, until cool. Rub away the burned peel. Stem and seed the chiles and coarsely chop them. There should be about 1 cup.

In a medium saucepan, cover the black-eyed peas with cold water. Set over medium heat and bring to a simmer. Cook 10 minutes, stir in the salt, and cook another 10 to 12 minutes, or until just tender. Drain. *The peas can be cooked up to 1 day ahead. Refrigerate, covered.*

In a large skillet over low heat, warm the olive oil. Add the green onions, garlic, and cumin and cook, covered, stirring once or twice, for 4 minutes. Stir in the chiles and cook 2 minutes. Stir in the black-eyed peas and the rice and cook, covered, stirring once or twice, until heated through. Adjust the seasoning and serve.

serves 6 to 8

texmati pilaf

Texmati rice is the Texas-grown version of the fragrant staple grain of India, basmati. We have concocted the following pink and flavorful hybrid, a cross between classic arroz mexicano and the authentic Indian preparation, in order to take advantage of the brand-new, very old, Texas agricultural product. If you (like us) have a soft spot for gloppy "Spanish rice," be warned—this is not that: The texture is fluffy and the grains are separate.

1 cup white Texmati rice, rinsed in
    a strainer
1 juicy ripe medium tomato (about
    ½ pound), stemmed, cored, and
    chunked
½ cup chopped onion
2 garlic cloves, peeled and chopped
1 medium jalapeño chile, stemmed
    and chopped

1 teaspoon salt
About 1½ cups chicken broth,
    homemade or canned
3 tablespoons olive oil
1 cup frozen peas, defrosted and
    well drained (optional)

In a bowl, combine the Texmati rice with hot tap water to cover and let stand for 25 minutes. Drain well in a strainer, shaking off as much water as possible.

In a blender, combine the tomato, onions, garlic, jalapeño, and salt and blend until smooth. Stir in enough chicken broth to equal 2¼ cups.

In a small saucepan over medium-low heat, heat the olive oil. When it is hot, stir in the Texmati rice. Cook, stirring and scraping the rice if it sticks to the pan, for 2 minutes, or until the grains are opaque. Stir in the tomato mixture (there will be sizzling) and bring just to a simmer, stirring once. Cover the pan, lower the heat, and cook undisturbed for 22 minutes. Remove the pan from the heat, scatter the peas, if you are using them, over the surface of the rice and let stand, covered, for 5 minutes.

Stir the peas into the rice and serve immediately.

serves 6

calico corn

This is an easy and colorful little side dish, one that goes with all manner of Southwestern entrées. The zesty seasonings add zip to canned hominy and canned or frozen corn, and the results are speedy and good to eat.

½ stick (4 tablespoons) unsalted butter

1 large heavy sweet red pepper, stemmed, cored, and finely diced

2 garlic cloves, peeled and minced

1 fresh jalapeño chile, stemmed and minced

3 cups corn kernels, canned or defrosted frozen, well drained

1 20-ounce can white or yellow hominy, drained (about 2 cups)

4 green onions, trimmed and sliced (about ⅔ cup)

½ teaspoon salt

In a large skillet over medium heat, melt the butter. Stir in the sweet red pepper, garlic, and jalapeño and cook, stirring once or twice, for 5 minutes. Stir in the corn, hominy, green onions, and salt and cook, covered, stirring once or twice, until heated through, about 4 minutes. Adjust the seasoning and serve immediately.

serves 6

grilled corn on the cob with lime butter
and chili powder

This is our home version of the widely popular Mexican street snack—ears of grilled corn served, impaled, Popsicle-style, on sturdy sticks. When we run across heavy, pointed dowels (usually in craft shops, and then only rarely) we stock up. Ordinary wooden skewers are too flimsy, and if we're out of dowels we just skip the sticks altogether. (One disastrously rustic attempt to gather and launder fallen twigs from the yard is better forgotten.) The point, after all, is the sweet, hot, tender corn, dripping with lime butter, aflame with chili powder. In summer we often have a yard full of well-dressed guests, strolling among Martina's roses, gnawing on ears of corn—what a sight! (In our dietary version of this, we omit the butter and offer fresh lime wedges, which are squeezed onto the corn, to be followed by a shake of chili powder.)

1 stick (4 ounces) unsalted butter, softened
Finely grated zest (colored peel) of 2 limes

6 ears of sweet, tender corn, shucked and impaled (if you have them) on sturdy, pointed dowels
3 tablespoons corn oil
Mild chili powder blend, in a shaker

In a small bowl, cream together the butter and lime zest. *The butter can be prepared up to 3 days ahead and refrigerated, well covered. Soften it to room temperature before using it.*

Preheat a gas grill (medium-high) or light a charcoal fire and let it burn down until the coals are evenly white. Position a rack about 6 inches above the heat source. Brush the ears of corn with the corn oil, lay them on the grill with the dowels extending over the side of the grill away from the flame, and cover the grill. Cook the corn, turning it once or twice, until it is hot and steaming and lightly marked by the grill, 4 to 6 minutes.

Serve, offering lime butter for spreading and chili powder for shaking onto the corn.

serves 6

perfectly lumpy mashed potatoes

Unlike lumpy gravy, lumpy mashed potatoes are a good thing, and we go just a bit out of our way when we make these to ensure that there are plenty of lumps. Idaho baking potatoes make the best mashed spuds; leaving the peels on adds texture, fiber, and nutrient value, as well as saving time, but feel free to peel if you prefer.

4½ pounds baking potatoes, peeled if desired, or if not, well scrubbed, cut into 2-inch chunks
4 teaspoons salt plus more to taste
1½ cups milk

¾ stick (6 tablespoons) unsalted butter
1 teaspoon freshly ground black pepper plus more to taste

In a large heavy pan, cover the potatoes with cold water. Stir in 2 teaspoons of salt, set over medium heat, and bring to a boil. Lower the heat slightly, partially cover, and cook, stirring once or twice, until the potatoes are very tender, about 25 minutes.

Meanwhile, in a small saucepan, bring the milk just to a simmer. Stir in the butter, 2 teaspoons of salt, and 1 teaspoon of freshly ground black pepper. Cover the saucepan and remove it from the heat. Drain the potatoes and return them to the pan. Mash the potatoes (leave some lumps). Return the pan to low heat and whisk in the heated milk mixture. Beat the potatoes with a wooden spoon (or an electric mixer) until they are light and fluffy. Adjust the seasoning and serve immediately.

For *Mashed Sweet Potatoes,* substitute an equal weight of peeled, chunked yams.

serves 8

calabacitas con crema
(sautéed zucchini with green chiles and cream)

Zucchini are the shmoos (if you are familiar with these self-effacing, utterly accommodating, edible creatures from Al Capp's *L'il Abner* comics) of the vegetable world. With little effort on the part of the cook they agreeably transform themselves into any number of tasty things to eat. This easy sauté, flavored and lightly fired with chopped green chiles, is our all-purpose green vegetable side dish for many meals. If your green chiles include some that have partially (or entirely) ripened to red, they'll add a welcome color accent too.

3 long green chiles
3 tablespoons unsalted butter
½ cup finely diced onion
2 garlic cloves, minced
½ teaspoon dried oregano,
    crumbled

2 pounds (6 medium) zucchini,
    scrubbed, trimmed, halved
    lengthwise, and sliced crosswise
    into ½-inch-thick pieces
½ teaspoon salt
½ cup Crema (page 254) or crème
    fraîche

In the open flame of a gas burner or under a preheated broiler, roast the long green chiles, turning them, until they are lightly but evenly charred. Steam the chiles in a paper bag, or in a bowl, covered with a plate, until cool. Rub away the burned peel. Stem and seed the chiles and coarsely chop them. There should be about ½ cup.

In a large skillet over medium heat, melt the butter. Add the onions, garlic, and oregano and cook, stirring once or twice, until lightly colored, about 6 minutes. Stir in the zucchini, season with the salt, and cook, stirring and tossing often, for 3 minutes. Stir in the green chiles and cook another 3 to 4 minutes, or until the zucchini is almost tender. Stir in the crema, lower the heat, cover the skillet, and cook, stirring once or twice, until the sauce has thickened, about 3 minutes. Adjust the seasoning and serve immediately.

serves 4 to 6

grilled vegetable platter

Grilling lightly oiled vegetables adds a world of flavor, texture, and color to them. Consider this recipe an outline to which you can add or subtract, depending on what you find in the market. The vegetables make a colorful side dish for any number of grilled main courses, but they are so good we often enjoy them as a light main course on their own, accompanied by nothing more than a pepper mill and a hunk or two of Texas Toast (page 189). The wood chips are optional but nice if you like an especially smoky flavor (we do).

12 red-skinned new potatoes (about 1½ pounds), well scrubbed

4 teaspoons salt plus salt to taste for the finished platter

2 medium eggplants (about 2 pounds total), trimmed and sliced ½-inch thick

2 cups mesquite or hickory wood smoking chips

About ½ cup olive oil

3 medium zucchini, well scrubbed, trimmed, and cut into long ½-inch-thick slices

3 medium yellow squash, well scrubbed, trimmed, and cut into long ½-inch-thick slices

3 large heavy sweet peppers (red, yellow, orange, or a combination), stemmed, cored, and quartered

3 large tomatoes, ripe but firm, halved horizontally

12 to 16 large green onions, trimmed (leave no more than 3 inches of green top)

2 tablespoons minced fresh rosemary or marjoram or ¼ cup chopped fresh basil (optional)

In a medium pot, cover the potatoes with cold water. Stir in 2 teaspoons of salt, set over medium heat, and bring to a boil. Cook, uncovered, stirring once or twice, until the potatoes are just tender, 8 to 9 minutes. Drain them immediately and cool them to room temperature.

In a colander set over a plate, sprinkle the eggplant slices with 2 teaspoons of salt. Let them stand at room temperature for 1 hour, turning them once or twice (the eggplant will exude some of its juices). Wipe off the excess salt and pat the eggplant dry.

Soak the wood chips in water for at least 30 minutes.

Preheat a gas grill (medium) or light a charcoal fire and let it burn down until the coals are evenly white. Drain the wood chips, scatter them over the grill stones or coals, and cover the grill. When the chips are smoking, position the rack about 6 inches above the heat source. Brush the vegetables lightly and evenly with the olive oil. Arrange the vegetables on the rack, cover the grill, and cook, adjusting the positions of the vegetables on the rack to create attractive markings, and turning them once or twice, until they are lightly browned and tender, 4 to 5 minutes per side. Transfer the vegetables to a large platter, sprinkle them with salt and the optional herbs, and serve hot, warm, or cool, accompanied by a pepper mill.

serves 6 to 8

corn bread, apple, and pine nut dressing
with fresh sage

Since the turkey always roasts more evenly and more quickly without a stuffing, we have gotten into the habit of cooking dressings outside of the turkey. With the same ingredients, of course, but baked apart from the turkey, in a second oven if you have one, or after the big bird comes out of your single oven, dressings made this way are crusty on the outside, moist and savory within. (A twelve-pound turkey will stay hot, tented with foil and uncarved, for at least an hour.) This favorite dressing combines a number of Southwestern ingredients (FYI, excellent apples grow throughout Texas and New Mexico) and is also good with ham, roast beef, or pork.

¾ cup pine nuts
¾ stick (6 tablespoons) unsalted
    butter
3 cups coarsely diced onion
1½ teaspoons dried thyme,
    crumbled
3 large baking apples (about 1½
    pounds total), such as Rome
    Beauty, cored and coarsely
    chunked

½ cup chopped fresh sage
1 teaspoon salt
2 recipes day-old Good Old Corn
    Bread (page 191), coarsely
    crumbled (about 13 cups)
2½ cups chicken broth, homemade
    or canned
2 teaspoons freshly ground black
    pepper

Preheat the oven to 375°F.

Spread the pine nuts in a single layer in a shallow metal baking dish (like a pie pan) and bake, stirring once or twice, until golden brown, 7 to 10 minutes. Transfer to a bowl and cool.

In a large skillet over medium heat, melt the butter. Add the onions and thyme and cook, covered, stirring once or twice, for 5 minutes. Add the apples and cook, covered, stirring once or twice, for 5 minutes. Remove from the heat, stir in the sage and salt, and cool to room temperature. *The dressing can be prepared to this point several hours in advance.*

Position a rack in the middle of the oven and turn the oven up to 400°F.

Butter a large shallow baking dish (of about a 4-quart capacity). In a large bowl, thoroughly toss together the crumbled corn bread, apple mixture, and pine nuts. Stir in the chicken broth and the freshly ground black pepper and mix thoroughly. Spoon the dressing into the baking dish and bake uncovered for about 40 minutes, or until the top is lightly browned and the dressing is steaming.

serves 12

texas toast

The title of this recipe is a reverse tribute to the flabby brown 'n' serve rolls that masquerade under that very name in various restaurant chains around the country. *Our* Texas toast consists of crisp and smoky slabs of grilled country bread served up piping hot and lavishly spread with a zesty garlic butter. If you, like us, cook on a fast-heating gas grill, you'll find yourself firing it up to prepare nothing more than the toast. This is also good—but not *as* good—done under the broiler.

1 stick (4 ounces) unsalted butter, softened
2 garlic cloves, peeled and crushed through a press
2 teaspoons hot pepper sauce

Pinch of salt
12 1½-inch-thick slices of day-old crusty country-style bread
About ⅓ cup olive oil

In a small bowl, stir together the butter, garlic, hot pepper sauce, and salt. *The butter can be prepared up to 3 days ahead and refrigerated, or frozen for up to 3 months. Soften it to room temperature before using it.*

Preheat a gas grill (medium-high). Brush both sides of the bread slices with the olive oil. Arrange the rack about 6 inches above the heat source and arrange the bread on the rack. Cover and grill the bread, turning it once, until it is crisp and brown, 2 to 3 minutes per side. Spread one side of the toast generously with the softened butter mixture, pile it into a napkin-lined basket (which effectively gets garlic butter all over all sides of the toast), and serve immediately.

serves 6

double corn spoon bread with chiles and cheese

The Southwest is knee-deep in corn bread recipes, nearly all of them featuring corn, chiles, and cheese, along with whatever other personal punctuation marks the cook feels inclined to add. This is our contribution to the admirable abundance, one that we determined from the beginning to make as rich, moist, and devastatingly good as possible. Serve it as a meal's bread or in place of potatoes or other starch with chili, brisket, fried chicken, chilled gazpacho, etc., etc., or try it at brunch, teamed with eggs and bacon. When hot and freshly baked the bread is soft and spoonable; it firms as it cools and then cuts neatly into squares. Leftovers reheat beautifully in a microwave oven and, with a glass of cold milk, make a great midnight snack.

6 long green chiles

8 eggs, well beaten

2 16-ounce cans cream-style corn

2 cups (about 8 ounces) grated medium-sharp cheddar cheese or Monterey Jack cheese or a combination of both

1½ cups yellow cornmeal, preferably stone-ground

2 4-ounce jars chopped roasted red peppers, rinsed and drained

⅔ cup cultured buttermilk

½ cup sugar

5 pickled jalapeño chiles, stemmed and minced (about ⅓ cup)

2 teaspoons baking powder

1½ teaspoons salt

1 teaspoon baking soda

In the open flame of a gas burner or under a preheated broiler, roast the long green chiles, turning them, until they are lightly but evenly charred. Steam the chiles in a paper bag, or in a bowl, covered with a plate, until cool. Rub away the burned peel. Stem and seed the chiles and coarsely chop them. There should be about 1 cup.

Position a rack in the middle of the oven and preheat the oven to 375°F.

Butter a 10- to 12-cup shallow casserole dish.

In a large bowl, whisk together the eggs, cream-style corn, and cheese. Stir in the cornmeal, green chiles, red peppers, and buttermilk. Add the sugar, jalapeños, baking powder, salt, and baking soda and mix well. Transfer the batter to the baking dish.

Bake for 35 to 40 minutes, or until puffed and just barely set in the center. Serve hot or warm.

serves 8 to 12

blueberry corn bread

We mostly make this corn bread in order to be able to make Blueberry Corn Bread Pudding with Custard Sauce (page 221), but in truth it makes good eating on its own. Try to make it with fresh berries—the frozen ones taste fine but discolor the batter to an unpleasant purplish-gray.

1¼ cups unbleached all-purpose
    flour
¾ cup yellow cornmeal, preferably
    stone-ground
¼ cup sugar
2 teaspoons baking powder
½ teaspoon salt
1 cup cultured buttermilk, at room
    temperature

1 egg, beaten
5 tablespoons unsalted butter,
    melted
1½ cups blueberries, preferably
    fresh, picked over, rinsed, and
    drained

Position a rack in the middle of the oven and preheat the oven to 400°F.
Grease an 8-inch-square baking pan.

In a large bowl, stir together the flour, cornmeal, sugar, baking powder, and salt. Add the buttermilk, egg, and melted butter and stir until partially combined. Add the berries and stir until just combined; do not overmix. Transfer the batter to the baking pan and spread it to the edges. Bake 20 to 25 minutes, or until the corn bread is firm, the edges are golden, and a tester inserted into the center comes out clean.

Cool 5 minutes on a rack before cutting. Serve hot or warm, or use the corn bread in bread pudding.

For *Good Old Corn Bread,* omit the blueberries and reduce the sugar to 2 tablespoons.

serves 8

masa biscuits

These jumbo, Texas-size biscuits include a generous measure of masa harina de maiz, the specially treated ground corn that is the basis for tortillas, tamales, and other Southwestern staples. Because the masa contains no gluten, these biscuits are remarkably tender, with a distinctive but subtle flavor like that of a corn tortilla. They're particularly good split, buttered, and topped with jalapeño jelly.

3¾ cups unbleached all-purpose flour
1½ cups masa harina de maiz (page 253)
2 tablespoons plus 1 teaspoon baking powder
1 teaspoon salt

1 stick (4 ounces) unsalted butter, well chilled and cut into small pieces
½ cup solid vegetable shortening, well chilled and cut into small pieces
2 cups cultured buttermilk, chilled

Position racks in the upper and middle thirds of the oven and preheat the oven to 450°F.

In a large bowl, stir together 3½ cups of the flour, the masa, baking powder, and salt. With a pastry cutter, blend in the butter and shortening until the mixture resembles a coarse and slightly lumpy meal. Stir in the buttermilk until a soft, crumbly dough is formed. Sprinkle the work surface with half of the remaining flour. Turn the dough out, gather it into a ball, and briefly knead it, just until it holds together. Flatten the dough, sprinkle it with the rest of the flour, and roll it out about 1 inch thick. With a round 3-inch cutter, form the biscuits, transferring them to 2 ungreased baking sheets and spacing them about 2 inches apart. Gather the scraps into a ball, roll it out to 1-inch thick, and cut out the remaining biscuits.

Set the baking sheets on the racks and bake about 15 minutes, exchanging the position of the sheets on the racks from top to bottom and from front to back at the halfway point, or until the biscuits are golden and crisp. Serve hot or warm.

makes 12

chiles rellenos fríos con guacamole
(cold fire-roasted long green chiles stuffed
with guacamole)

Well-stuffed long green chiles can be served cold, too, as this recipe illustrates. Two chiles can make a light main course for lunch or dinner on a sweltering day. We also use these as the edible garnish for a platter of Salpicón (page 120) or as one-vegetable plate on a large buffet of many different dishes. You may also stuff green chiles with a mayonnaise-bound salad of shrimp, crab, tuna, or chicken. Canned or defrosted whole green chiles are really not successful in this recipe.

8 or more large long green chiles	Pinch of salt
2 tablespoons red wine vinegar	⅓ cup olive oil
1 teaspoon prepared Dijon-style mustard	About 2 cups Guacamole (page 10)

In the open flame of a gas burner or under a preheated broiler, roast the long green chiles, turning them, until they are lightly but evenly charred. Steam the chiles in a paper bag, or in a bowl, covered with a plate, until cool. Rub away the burned peel.

Cut a long slit in one side of each chile and gently remove as many seeds as possible. In a small bowl, whisk together the vinegar, mustard, and salt. Slowly whisk in the olive oil; the dressing will thicken. In a shallow dish, pour the dressing into and over the chiles. Cover and let them marinate at room temperature, 1 hour.

Lift the chiles from the marinade, letting the excess drip back into the dish. Stuff each chile with about ¼ cup of the guacamole. Arrange the chiles on a platter, drizzle them with any remaining dressing, and serve immediately.

serves 4 to 8

chiles rellenos
(battered-dipped cheese-stuffed long green chiles)

The real test of a successful Southwestern home cook is a batch of properly made chiles rellenos. These fire-roasted long green chiles, stuffed with cheese, dipped into an egg batter and deep-fried, are so utterly simple that even a slight misstep renders them ruined—not inedible, mind you—but a failure from a chile relleno connoisseur's point of view nonetheless. Since they are tricky, but delicious, most cooks abdicate, preferring to enjoy them in restaurants only. Others, the brave, set out to become devastatingly good at relleno making. It's a dish where practice makes perfect, and we humbly feel we have worked out all the bugs. Two tips up front: Look for long green chiles that are large, relatively straight, and thick-walled; and fire-roast more than the eight needed for the recipe. Inevitably during the stuffing process one or more chiles get torn too badly to use, and you'll be glad to have backups. Though chiles rellenos can be eaten plain (especially recommended the first time you taste them, to appreciate their simplicity), we have suggested two sauces that can be used as optional embellishment.

8 or more large long green chiles
8 ounces Monterey Jack cheese or
    medium-sharp cheddar cheese or
    a combination of both, cut into
    ½-inch strips
About 4 cups corn oil
6 eggs, at room temperature
2 tablespoons water

⅓ cup plus 1 tablespoon
    unbleached all-purpose flour
½ teaspoon salt
Ranchero Sauce (page 164) or the
    sauce for Enchiladas de Pollo
    Verdes (page 38), heated to
    simmering

In the open flame of a gas burner or under a preheated broiler, roast the long green chiles, turning them, until they are lightly but evenly charred. Steam the chiles in a paper bag, or in a bowl, covered with a plate, until cool. Rub away the burned peel.

Beginning at the stem end, cut a 2-inch slit in the side of each chile. With the tip of a finger, scrape out as many seeds as you can without enlarging the slit or otherwise tearing the chile (a few seeds left behind don't matter). Carefully slip a strip of cheese into the slit of each chile, pushing the cheese as far down into the tips as you can without tearing the chiles. Close the slits over the cheese. *The chiles can be prepared to this point 1 hour ahead. Cover them and refrigerate.*

In one or two wide deep skillets, warm 1 inch of corn oil over medium heat. Meanwhile, separate the eggs, transferring the yolks to a medium-size wide dish about 5 inches deep and the whites to a large bowl. Whisk the water into the yolks, then whisk in the flour and salt. Beat the whites until soft peaks form. Stir ⅓ of the whites into the yolk mixture to lighten it; then gently fold in the remaining whites. Do not overmix—streaks of white are acceptable.

When the oil has reach 375°F, dip a stuffed chile, slit-side up, into the batter. With a pancake turner, carefully transfer the chile to the hot oil, slit-side up. Immediately baste the batter on the top of the relleno with hot oil to seal it. Repeat this with the rest of the rellenos, working in batches if necessary, and fry them, turning once, until the batter is puffed and golden, about 2½ minutes per side. With a slotted spoon, transfer the rellenos in a single layer to absorbent paper. They can be kept warm in a 200°F oven until all have been fried. Serve immediately, napped with ranchero sauce or the green enchilada sauce, if desired.

serves 4

chapter eleven

cool and crunchy
salads and relishes

All that salsa, plus the lettuce, tomato, and onion in our tacos, may seem to be all the veggies a west Texan needs, and in truth, in a land where water is an ever-diminishing commodity and where the weather is one of extremes, tender vegetables, greens, and delicate herbs are not as commonly found as, say, dried beans. Still, this is modern America, and produce from all over the country finds its way here, and as modern cooks we want to eat lighter and healthier. Thus, cool salads and other pale green things, even lettuce salads and cranberry relish, turn up on our tables—usually, we note, with a Southwestern touch or two.

edythe may's mango salad

This recipe was a favorite of Park's paternal grandmother, Edythe May, as well as of almost every other cook in El Paso, it seems—it's a real local specialty, and it turns up on menus ranging from chili and beans to the Thanksgiving turkey. (It helps to remember that while Texas is West, it is also South, where such "congealed" salads abound.) For a buffet we pre-portion the salad, putting each square on a separate small lettuce leaf. These portions are then arranged on a large platter, making it easy for guests to help themselves. Some folks like the salad topped with sour cream, brown sugar, and coconut, but the Kerrs take it plain.

1 29-ounce can mangoes	8 ounces cream cheese, softened
3 3-ounce packages lemon flavor gelatin	2 tablespoons fresh lime juice
	Leaves of lettuce (optional)

Drain the mangoes, combining the juice with enough water to equal 3 cups liquid. In a small saucepan over medium heat, bring the liquid to a boil. In a large bowl, combine the boiling liquid and lemon flavor gelatin and stir until dissolved.

In a food processor, combine the mangoes and cream cheese and process until smooth. Whisk the mango mixture into the gelatin. Stir in the lime juice. Pour the mixture into a 9- by 13-inch pan and refrigerate until firm, about 5 hours. *The salad can be prepared up to 1 day ahead.*

Cut the salad into squares and serve, placing each square on a lettuce leaf, if desired.

serves 12

jalapeño-pineapple coleslaw

This cool, crunchy, tangy, and slightly *picante* salad turns up often on our table. It's so easy to make and it goes with so many things, we think you'll soon find it indispensable too. The amount of jalapeño called for here makes the salad only slightly fiery—adjust things upward or downward as you please. A couple of ripe mangoes can be pitted, peeled, and diced and used in place of the pineapple.

1 cup mayonnaise
1 cup sour cream or plain yogurt
5 pickled jalapeño chiles, stemmed
    and minced (about ½ cup)
3 tablespoons prepared Dijon-style
    mustard
3 tablespoons sugar
2 tablespoons fresh lemon juice
½ teaspoon salt

1 medium white cabbage
    (about 1½ pounds), cored and finely
    shredded (about 8 cups)
Half a large ripe pineapple, cored,
    peeled, and cut into ½-inch cubes
    (about 2 cups)
3 green onions, trimmed and sliced
    (about ½ cup)

In a large bowl, whisk together the mayonnaise, sour cream, jalapeños, mustard, sugar, lemon juice, and salt. Add the cabbage and pineapple and stir well. Cover the slaw and refrigerate it for at least 1 hour. *The coleslaw can be prepared up to 1 day ahead.*

Stir in the green onions and adjust the seasoning just before serving.

serves 8

texas three-bean salad

Of course the usual kind of sweet-and-sour three-bean salad gets made all the time in Texas (it's great with a big grilled steak), but we like this version, made entirely with dried beans, equally well. (We have also, on occasion, added about ½ pound crisp-cooked sliced green or wax beans, particularly when we have found ourselves in the position of feeding traditional three-bean salad eaters.) The black beans are cooked separately to prevent their discoloring the pintos and the chick-peas.

1 cup dried black beans,
  picked over
1 cup dried chick-peas, picked over
1 cup dried pinto beans, picked
  over
3½ teaspoons salt
⅓ cup balsamic vinegar
3 pickled jalapeño chiles, stemmed
  and minced (about ⅓ cup)

1 large egg yolk, at room
  temperature
2 garlic cloves, peeled and minced
1 teaspoon ground cumin
½ cup corn oil
½ cup olive oil
1 cup coarsely diced red onion

In a medium bowl, combine the black beans with enough water to cover by at least 3 inches. In a large bowl, combine the chick-peas and pinto beans with enough water to cover by at least 3 inches. Soak the beans for 24 hours.

Drain the beans. In a small saucepan, cover the black beans with fresh cold water. In a medium saucepan, cover the pintos and chick-peas with fresh cold water. Set the pans over medium heat and bring to a boil. Adjust the heat and simmer the beans uncovered, stirring them occasionally, for 20 minutes. Stir 1 teaspoon of salt into the black beans and 2 teaspoons of salt into the pinto bean mixture and simmer both pans of beans another 15 to 20 minutes, or until they are just tender. Drain the beans and transfer them to a large bowl.

Meanwhile, in a food processor, combine the balsamic vinegar, jalapeños, egg yolk, garlic, cumin, and ½ teaspoon of salt. Process until smooth. With the motor running, add the corn and olive oils in a slow, steady stream. The dressing will thicken.

Pour the dressing over the warm beans and toss thoroughly. *The salad can be prepared up to 1 day ahead. Cover it and refrigerate. Return it to room temperature before serving it.*

Stir in the red onions and adjust the seasoning just before serving.

serves 8

roasted new potato salad with green chiles

The salad is spectacular made with freshly fire-roasted chiles, delicious prepared with defrosted roasted chiles (homemade or purchased), but only acceptable when canned green chiles are used. Roasting the potatoes makes the salad earthier and seems to intensify the potato flavor, but they can be boiled if you prefer.

4 long green chiles
2½ pounds red-skinned new
    potatoes, well scrubbed and
    patted dry
3 tablespoons corn oil

½ cup olive oil
3 tablespoons white wine vinegar
¾ teaspoon salt
⅓ cup chopped sweet red onion

In the open flame of a gas burner or under a preheated broiler, roast the long green chiles, turning them, until they are lightly but evenly charred. Steam the chiles in a paper bag, or in a bowl, covered with a plate, until cool. Rub away the burned peel. Stem and seed the chiles and coarsely chop them. There should be about ⅔ cup.

Position a rack in the middle of the oven and preheat the oven to 400°F.

In a jelly roll pan large enough to hold them in a single layer, toss the potatoes with the corn oil. Bake the potatoes, occasionally stirring and rolling them in the pan, until they are tender and the peels are crisp, about 45 minutes. Remove the pan of potatoes from the oven and set it on a rack.

When the potatoes are just cool enough to handle, cut them in half. In a large mixing bowl, toss together the warm potatoes, green chiles, olive oil, vinegar, and salt. *If necessary the recipe can be prepared to this point up to 3 hours ahead. Cover it tightly and store it at room temperature for best texture.*

Just before serving, stir in the red onions and adjust the seasoning.

serves 8

ensalada de nopalitos
(prickly pear cactus pad salad)

It will probably not encourage you to know that during droughts Texas cattlemen roam their fields, burning the spines off the pads of prickly pear cacti with flamethrowers in order to give their livestock something nourishing and moist to eat. In our experience most folks throw up a high fence between animal fodder and food, particularly where spines are involved. If we add that during cooking nopales exude a sticky juice similar to that of okra, we will probably lose the rest of the room. Still, when properly cooked (to retain some texture but banish most of that juice), nopales (called nopalitos when cut into julienne) have a pleasantly green vegetable flavor that we love.

Whole tender young cactus pads are showing up grilled on many New Southwestern restaurant menus, an agreeable way to sample this exotic produce. This zesty, traditional Mexican salad, in which the cactus pads are combined with pickled jalapeños and tangy cheese and dressed with lime juice and olive oil, is also a great introduction. Though we find some uses for bottled nopalitos, for the salad they really must be fresh. The green onion tops with which the nopalitos are cooked are said to help remove the sticky juices.

1 large heavy sweet red pepper
4½ teaspoons salt
1 pound nopales, spines removed,
    tough edges trimmed, cut into
    long ¼-inch strips
Tops of 4 green onions
6 to 8 pickled jalapeño chiles,
    stemmed and cut into julienne
3 tablespoons fresh lime juice
2 tablespoons olive oil

2 juicy ripe medium tomatoes,
    trimmed and cut into wedges
1 buttery-ripe black-skinned
    avocado, pitted and cut into thin
    unpeeled wedges
1 small red onion, peeled and sliced
    into thin rings
4 ounces crumbled soft white
    cheese, such as feta cheese or
    goat cheese

In the open flame of a gas burner or under a preheated broiler, roast the red pepper, turning it, until the peel is evenly charred. In a closed paper bag or in a bowl covered with a plate, steam the pepper until cool. Rub away the blackened skin, stem and core the pepper, and cut the flesh into julienne.

Over high heat, bring a medium pan of water to a boil. Stir in 2 teaspoons of salt and the nopalitos. Cook for 3 minutes, then drain and rinse the nopalitos under cold running water. Fill the pan with fresh cold water, set over medium heat, and bring to a boil. Stir in 2 teaspoons of salt, the nopalitos, and green onion tops and bring to a boil. Lower the heat and simmer about 10 minutes, or until the nopalitos are tender and no longer slippery. Drain and transfer them to a bowl of iced water. When they are cool, drain thoroughly.

In a large bowl toss together the roasted red pepper, nopalitos, and pickled jalapeños. Add the lime juice, olive oil, and ½ teaspoon of salt and toss again. Adjust the seasoning.

Arrange the nopalito mixture on a serving plate. Top with the tomato wedges, avocado wedges, and red onion slices. Scatter the crumbled cheese over all and serve immediately.

serves 6 to 8

avocado-buttermilk salad dressing

This thick and creamy dressing is delicious dolloped onto crisp greens (like romaine, endive, or watercress). It can also be used to dress cold poached shrimp, chicken, or fish.

2 buttery-ripe black-skinned avocados, (about 1 pound), pitted and
peeled
2 green onions, chopped (about
⅓ cup)
½ cup mayonnaise

3 tablespoons lemon juice
1 teaspoon salt
½ teaspoon freshly ground black
pepper
1½ cups cultured buttermilk

In a food processor, combine the avocado, green onions, mayonnaise, lemon juice, salt, and freshly ground black pepper and process until smooth. Add the buttermilk and process until combined. Transfer to a container and cover with plastic wrap, pressing the film onto the surface of the dressing. Refrigerate until serving. *The dressing can be prepared up to 1 day ahead.*

makes about 3½ cups

jalapeño-cranberry relish

Just a touch of Southwestern heat adds a whole new flavor dimension to classic raw cranberry relish. Since we make this often, not just for Thanksgiving, the recipe has a modest yield, but it doubles easily if there's a crowd on the way. And don't limit this zesty relish to the holiday season: It's a delicious surprise alongside grilled beef, pork, or chicken at the height of summer. We always put a bag or two of loose berries away in the back of the freezer so we can have it anytime.

1 12-ounce bag cranberries, picked over, rinsed, and drained
1 large unpeeled navel orange, scrubbed, cut into thin wedges, and seeded

1 medium fresh jalapeño chile, stemmed and chopped
About 1 cup sugar
2 tablespoons Triple Sec
1 tablespoon fresh lime juice

In a food processor, in two batches, chop together the cranberries, orange wedges, and jalapeño.

In a medium bowl, stir together the cranberry mixture, ¾ cup of the sugar, the Triple Sec, and lime juice. *Cover and refrigerate for at least 1 hour. The relish can be prepared up to 1 day ahead.* The relish may require additional sugar, to taste, after standing.

serves 6 to 8

home-smoked chipotles

Chipotles adobado—smoked red-ripe jalapeños packed in a sharp tomato sauce—are one of our favorite ingredients and a wonderful condiment and we use them often. Once we ran across a mound of fresh red jalapeños and on impulse decided to make our own chipotles. We used a simple water smoker, and the results were fresh, colorful, and astonishingly good. Grow your own jalapeños, ask the produce man to sort out some red ones for you, or take home green ones and ripen them yourself. Note that for this recipe chile paste from a jar is preferable to homemade.

3 chunks of mesquite or hickory
  smoking wood
1¼ pounds red-ripe jalapeño chiles,
  with stems
½ cup red chile paste, preferably
  Santa Cruz brand or substitute
  homemade

¼ cup water
2 tablespoons tomato paste
2 tablespoons cider vinegar
1 tablespoon brown sugar
1 garlic clove, peeled and forced
  through a press
¼ teaspoon salt

Soak the wood chunks in water for 2 hours. Set up an electric water smoker outdoors in a place shielded from the wind.

Arrange the jalapeños in a single layer in a disposable foil pan just large enough to fit on a smoker rack. Drain the wood chunks. Place them in the smoker and set the basin of water in place according to the smoker manufacturer's directions. Set the pan of jalapeños on the lower rack of the smoker and set the cover in place. Smoke for 2 to 2½ hours, depending on the wind, weather, and smoker you use, or until the jalapeños are soft.

Transfer the smoked chiles and any juices from the foil pan to a medium saucepan. Stir in the chile paste, water, tomato paste, vinegar, brown sugar, garlic, and salt. Set the saucepan over medium heat and bring the mixture it to a simmer. Cook, stirring once or twice (avoid breaking up the chipotles if possible), until the sauce is very thick, about 15 minutes. Cool to room temperature. *The chipotles can be stored, covered, in the refrigerator for up to 5 days.*

makes about 3 cups

chapter twelve

sweet finales
desserts, candies, and treats

Texans, at birth, seem to come equipped with a few more sweet teeth than other folks have. Grand desserts of all shapes, sizes, and flavors, some of American and others of Mexican origin, are as common in Texas as tumbleweeds and tall tales. Perhaps it is Texas's proximity to the Deep South, possibly it is just a natural extension of every Texan's innate gift for hospitality, or maybe something a little sweet is just what the palate needs after a meal of smoke and fire and spice. Whatever the reason, a big, sweet, old-fashioned dessert (or two or three) turns up on the Texas table with the same agreeable regularity as the smile of welcome at the door. Have another cup of coffee, darlin', and cut yourself another piece of pie.

"aunt hazel millican's" sweet chocolate cake

Park and Monica have fond memories of journeying to east Texas to visit Aunt Hazel and Uncle Julian's place on Pig Foot Creek. Julian would fry up a mess of catfish and hush puppies, everyone would drink ice tea from tin cans (the Millicans were early recyclers), and Aunt Hazel would proudly whip up a multilayer version of "her" famous chocolate cake. She was not unique among Texas cooks in believing this classic cake a personal invention. It has been baked and enjoyed in these parts for so long, it's a natural mistake to make.

Discovered in a Dallas newspaper by a savvy marketing person from General Foods (the makers of the all-important German's Sweet Chocolate), the cake is in fact a regional specialty that was tested, revised, and promoted by General Foods into a national phenomenon. Baking it as a sheet (or sheath, as we Texans say) cake simplifies the process somewhat and makes it easier to take along to ice-cream socials, covered-dish suppers, and other get-togethers, none of which would be half as much fun without Sweet Chocolate Cake for dessert.

CAKE
2 cups unbleached all-purpose flour
1 teaspoon baking soda
½ teaspoon salt
4 ounces Baker's German's sweet
  chocolate, chopped
½ cup boiling water
2 sticks (8 ounces) unsalted butter,
  softened
2 cups sugar
4 eggs, separated

1 teaspoon vanilla extract
1 cup cultured buttermilk

FROSTING
1 12-ounce can evaporated milk
1½ cups sugar
4 egg yolks, slightly beaten
1½ sticks (6 ounces) unsalted butter
1½ teaspoons vanilla extract
2 cups flaked, sweetened coconut
1½ cups chopped pecans

FOR THE CAKE
Position a rack in the middle of the oven and preheat the oven to 350°F. Grease and flour a 9- by 13-inch baking pan, preferably of metal. (If using glass, reduce the oven temperature to 325°F.)

In a medium bowl, sift together the flour, baking soda, and salt. In a small bowl, mix together the chocolate and the water and stir until the chocolate is melted. In a large bowl, cream together the butter and sugar until fluffy. Beat in the egg yolks. Stir in the vanilla extract and chocolate. Beat the flour mixture and the buttermilk alternately into the chocolate mixture. In a clean medium bowl, whisk the egg whites until stiff peaks form. Fold the whites into the batter. Pour the batter into the baking pan and bake 55 minutes, or until the cake springs back when lightly pressed in the center. Cool it completely on a rack.

FOR THE FROSTING

In a medium saucepan, combine the evaporated milk, sugar, egg yolks, butter, and vanilla extract. Set over medium heat and cook, stirring often, until thickened, about 12 minutes. Remove from the heat, stir in the coconut and pecans, and cool, beating occasionally, until the frosting is thick enough to spread.

Frost the cake with the icing. Store the cake, loosely covered, at room temperature until serving.

serves 9

peach cobbler

Settlers first brought peaches to the West in cans, and there remains in El Paso a fondness for tinned fruit that is all out of proportion, especially considering the abundant and spectacular fresh peaches grown all over Texas. Some of the best come from Fredericksburg. (Norma always stopped there for a bushel basketful on her way home from driving Monica to college in Austin.) During fresh peach season, we eat our fill of this cobbler, serving it warm or cool, with heavy cream, whipped cream, sour cream, or vanilla ice cream, depending on our mood and the rest of the meal. Amaretto replaces vanilla extract and seems to make the peaches taste peachier.

FILLING
4 pounds (about 14 medium) ripe,
    juicy peaches
1 cup sugar
½ cup unbleached all-purpose flour
2 tablespoons fresh lemon juice
2 tablespoons Amaretto

TOPPING
2¼ cups unbleached all-purpose
    flour
¼ cup plus 2 tablespoons sugar

3 teaspoons baking powder
Pinch of salt
½ stick (4 tablespoons) unsalted
    butter, well chilled and cut into
    small pieces
¼ cup solid vegetable shortening,
    well chilled and cut into small
    pieces
1 egg, well beaten
Finely minced zest of 2 lemons
1¼ cups cultured buttermilk

Position a rack in the upper third of the oven and preheat the oven to 400°F.

FOR THE FILLING
Peel the peaches if necessary by dropping them a few at a time into a pot of boiling water, leaving them for 1 minute, and then transferring them to a bowl of iced water. The peels will then slip off easily. Pit and slice the peaches. In a bowl, stir together the peaches, sugar, flour, lemon juice, and Amaretto. Transfer the peaches to a 9- by 13-inch baking dish and bake 20 minutes.

FOR THE TOPPING

In a bowl, stir together the flour, ¼ cup of sugar, baking powder, and salt. Cut in the butter and shortening until the mixture is coarse and crumbly. Stir in the egg, lemon zest, and buttermilk until a soft dough forms; do not overmix.

Drop the topping by large dollops evenly over the surface of the hot peaches. Sprinkle the topping evenly with the remaining 2 tablespoons of sugar. Return the cobbler to the oven and bake another 15 to 20 minutes, or until the topping is puffed and golden and the filling is bubbling. Let stand on a rack and serve hot, warm, or cool.

serves 8

a big sunday dinner

Norma's Iced Mango Tea with Mint (page 243)

Salsa Shrimp Cocktails (page 21)

Texas Party Brisket (page 118)
Calico Corn (page 182)
Calabacitas con Crema (page 185)
Perfectly Lumpy Mashed Potatoes (page 184)
Masa Biscuits (page 192) with Butter and Hot Pepper Jelly

Grandma Lora Belle Godwin's Lemon-Buttermilk Pie (page 214)
"Aunt Hazel Millican's" Sweet Chocolate Cake (page 208)

---

sweet potato spice rack pie

This is an old-fashioned pie, with a pinch of this and a pinch of that from the spice rack, plus a splash of red-eye from the jug on the porch. Serve each slice, if you like, with a dollop of lightly sweetened, bourbon-spiked whipped cream.

2 medium sweet potatoes (about 1¼ pounds total)
3 eggs
1 cup packed light brown sugar
½ teaspoon ground cinnamon
½ teaspoon freshly grated nutmeg
½ teaspoon ground ginger
½ teaspoon salt
¼ teaspoon ground cloves

¼ teaspoon ground allspice
¼ teaspoon ground cardamom
¼ teaspoon ground coriander
¾ cup whipping cream
½ cup half-and-half
3 tablespoons bourbon
1 tablespoon vanilla extract
1 unbaked 9-inch pie shell
(page 213), chilled

Preheat the oven to 400°F. Pierce each sweet potato twice with the tines of a fork and bake until very tender, about 1 hour. Cool them to room temperature, peel them, and mash enough sweet potato to equal 1¾ cups.

Position a rack in the middle level of the oven and set a baking sheet on the rack. Preheat the oven to 350°F.

In a food processor, combine the sweet potato, eggs, light brown sugar, cinnamon, nutmeg, ginger, salt, cloves, allspice, cardamom, and coriander and process briefly. Add the whipping cream, half-and-half, bourbon, and vanilla extract and process again, pausing once to scrape the work bowl, until smooth. Pour the filling into the pie shell, set it on the heated baking sheet, and bake 45 to 50 minutes, or until a tester inserted into the center comes out clean. Cool completely on a rack before cutting.

1 9-inch pie, serving 6 to 8

pie pastry

2 cups unbleached all-purpose flour
⅛ teaspoon salt
5 tablespoons unsalted butter, well
   chilled and cut into small pieces

¼ cup solid vegetable shortening,
   well chilled and cut into small
   pieces
4 to 5 tablespoons water, chilled

In a food processor or a medium bowl, combine 1¾ cups of the flour and the salt. Cut in the butter and shortening until the mixture is coarse and crumbly. One tablespoon at a time, stir in enough water to form a soft dough.

Sprinkle the work surface with 2 tablespoons of the remaining flour. Turn the dough out onto the floured surface, gather it into a ball, and flatten the ball into a disk. Wrap it tightly in plastic and refrigerate it for 30 minutes.

Sprinkle the work surface with half of the remaining flour. Flatten the dough slightly on the floured surface, sprinkle it with the remaining flour, and roll it out about ¼-inch thick. Transfer the round of dough to a 9-inch pie pan. Trim the overhang, form an edge, and crimp it decoratively. Cover the formed pastry shell and refrigerate it at least 30 minutes. *The crust can be prepared to this point up to 1 day ahead.*

makes 1 9-inch single-crust pie shell

grandma lora belle godwin's lemon-buttermilk pie

Norma's mother, Lora Belle, is a wonderful cook and an extraordinary baker. Among the many sweet treats she has turned out for the family over the years is this sweet and lemony buttermilk custard pie, a simple variation on a traditional recipe. It probably takes a Texan to love this pie with its full complement (2 cups!) of sugar, and so we have reduced the quantity slightly, for those of you from the other forty-nine states.

1 stick (4 ounces) unsalted butter, softened
1¾ cups sugar
3 eggs, well beaten
⅓ cup unbleached all-purpose flour

1 cup cultured buttermilk, at room temperature
1 teaspoon lemon extract
Pinch of freshly grated nutmeg
1 9-inch unbaked pie shell (page 213)

Position a rack in the middle of the oven and set a baking sheet on the rack. Preheat the oven to 350°F.

In a medium bowl, cream the butter and sugar. Whisk in the eggs and flour. Mix in the buttermilk, lemon extract, and nutmeg. Pour the filling into the pie shell, set it on the heated baking sheet, and bake 45 to 50 minutes, or until it is puffed and brown and evenly set (but not firm) from edge to edge. Cool the pie completely to room temperature on a rack before cutting.

1 9-inch pie, serving 6

adobe pie

Considerably tastier than the combination of mud and straw for which it is named, this frozen ice-cream pie is beloved by both El Paso restaurateurs and hosts for its easy, do-ahead qualities, and beloved by El Paso diners for its rich, sweet coolness—ideal after a chile-fired main course.

1 cup chocolate cookie crumbs (we use Nabisco Famous Chocolate Wafers)

¼ cup sugar

½ stick (4 tablespoons) unsalted butter, melted

About ¾ pint premium butter pecan ice cream, softened

About 3 cups Kahlúa Chocolate Sauce (page 231)

About 1½ pints premium coffee ice cream, softened

1 cup whipping cream

3 tablespoons Kahlúa

In a medium bowl, stir together the chocolate cookie crumbs, sugar, and melted butter until the mixture is damp and crumbly. Pat this crust mixture evenly onto the bottom and up the sides of a 9-inch pie pan, using it all. Freeze the crust for 1 hour.

Spread the butter pecan ice cream in the pie crust in an even layer 1-inch thick. Spread 3 tablespoons of the Kahlúa Chocolate Sauce over the ice cream and return the pie to the freezer until the ice cream is firm. Spread the coffee ice cream over the pie, mounding it slightly in the center. Return the pie to the freezer. When the ice cream is solid, wrap the pie well in plastic wrap. *The pie can be kept in the freezer for up to 1 week.*

Soften the pie slightly in the refrigerator. Whip the cream to soft peaks and flavor it with the Kahlúa. Warm the remaining Kahlúa chocolate sauce. With a thin sharp knife dipped in hot water and wiped dry before each cut, slice the pie into 6 or 8 wedges. Transfer each wedge to a dessert plate, spoon about ⅓ cup chocolate sauce beside and over each, and garnish each with a dollop of whipped cream. Serve immediately.

1 9-inch pie, serving 6 to 8

mode à la pecan pie

This devastatingly good ice cream evolved from Park's creative but messy practice of chopping up a piece of leftover pecan pie and scattering it over a bowl of premium vanilla ice cream. Why not achieve the same thing on purpose? we wondered, and so came up with this recipe. If you're a purist you'll probably use homemade pie (the recipe printed on the back of the Karo syrup bottle is about perfect), but a good-quality frozen or bakery pie works well too.

4 cups whipping cream
3 cups half-and-half
8 egg yolks
1 cup sugar

2 teaspoons vanilla extract
5 slices of pecan pie, crust included,
    coarsely chopped

In a large heavy saucepan over medium heat, combine the whipping cream and half-and-half. Bring the mixture just to a boil.

Meanwhile, in a large bowl, whisk the egg yolks. Whisk in the sugar. Slowly dribble the hot cream into the egg mixture, whisking constantly. Return this mixture to the pan, set it over low heat, and cook, stirring constantly with a wooden spoon, until the mixture thickens sufficiently to heavily coat the back of the spoon and leaves a track when a finger is drawn across it, 4 to 5 minutes. Do not allow the mixture to boil. Transfer this custard to a large bowl, stir in the vanilla extract, and cool to room temperature. Cover with plastic wrap, pressing the film onto the surface of the custard, and refrigerate until very cold, preferably overnight.

Strain the mixture into the canister of an ice-cream maker and churn it according to the manufacturer's directions. Fold the chopped pecan pie into the finished ice cream until thoroughly distributed, cover, and freeze until serving. *The ice cream can be prepared up to 3 days ahead. Soften it slightly in the refrigerator if needed before scooping.*

makes about 3 quarts

border brownies

These cinnamon-, almond-, vanilla-, and orange-scented pecan brownies are from the chewy (as opposed to the fudgy or the cakey) school, rather soft and moist inside but slightly crusty outside, a wonderfully contrasting state of affairs. Mexican chocolate comes in "tablets" of varying weights, none adding up precisely to the amount called for here, which means you will need to use a scale. The brownies are not only good the day after they're baked, they're actually better than when fresh from the oven.

5 ounces Mexican chocolate, preferably Ibarra brand, chopped
¾ stick (6 tablespoons) unsalted
butter
1 cup unbleached all-purpose flour
(stir the flour with a fork, scoop
it into a dry-measure cup, and
sweep it level)
½ teaspoon baking soda

½ teaspoon salt
1 egg
½ cup packed light brown sugar
¼ cup sugar
2 tablespoons Triple Sec or other
orange liqueur
1 teaspoon vanilla extract
1 cup (about 4 ounces) coarsely
chopped pecans

Position a rack in the middle of the oven and preheat the oven to 350°F. Butter an 8- by 8-inch baking pan, preferably metal (if using glass, lower the oven temperature to 325°F).

In the top of a double boiler over hot (not simmering) water, melt together the chocolate and butter. Remove them from over the hot water and cool slightly. In a medium bowl, sift together the flour, baking soda, and salt.

In a medium bowl, whisk the egg. Whisk in the brown and white sugars until the mixture is thick and fluffy. Stir in the melted chocolate mixture, the Triple Sec, and vanilla extract. Sift in the flour mixture, stirring until just barely combined. Stir in the pecans. Transfer the batter to the baking pan and spread it to the edges. Bake about 25 minutes, or until a tester inserted about 1 inch from the edge of the pan comes out almost clean.

Cool the brownies on a rack to room temperature. Cut them into 9 equal pieces, remove them from the pan, and wrap them well. Let the brownies stand at room temperature 24 hours before serving.

makes 9

cowboy cookies

These oversized, overstuffed cookies provide a fistful of sweet eating for kids of all ages. The sombrero cookie jar in Norma and Bill's kitchen is never without a batch of these jumbo chippers, which, by the way, just aren't as much fun when they're baked regular size.

2 cups plus 2 tablespoons un-
    bleached all-purpose flour
1 teaspoon baking soda
1 teaspoon salt
1½ cups semisweet chocolate chunks
¾ cup granola (any variety)
¾ cup coarsely chopped pecans
¾ cup sundried cherries or golden
    raisins

¾ cup flaked, sweetened coconut
2 sticks (8 ounces) unsalted butter,
    softened
¾ cup packed light brown sugar
½ cup sugar
2 eggs
1 teaspoon vanilla extract

Position racks in the upper and lower thirds of the oven and preheat the oven to 325°F.

In a small bowl, thoroughly mix together the flour, baking soda, and salt. In a medium bowl, combine the chocolate chunks, granola, pecans, cherries, and coconut. In a large bowl, cream the butter. Beat in the brown and white sugars. One at a time, beat in the eggs; stir in the vanilla extract. Stir in the flour mixture. Add the chocolate chunk mixture and stir to combine thoroughly.

Using a ⅓-cup measure (some ice-cream scoops are this size, and for the best success at releasing the dough we recommend you use one) and working in batches, portion the dough onto two ungreased cookie sheets (sheets without sides will make removing oversized cookies easier), spacing them well apart. Flatten each ball of dough with the back of a fork into a round about ½-inch thick and about 3 inches in diameter.

Bake the cookies, exchanging the position of the cookie sheets on the racks from top to bottom and from front to back at the halfway point, for about 17 minutes. The cookies should be lightly browned and crisp at the edges, but not hard.

Cool the cookies on the sheets on a rack for 5 minutes before carefully transferring them with a wide spatula to absorbent paper. Cool them completely and store them, airtight. Repeat with the remaining dough. *The cookies can be baked up to 3 days ahead.*

makes 16 5-inch cookies

lemon-lime cookies

These crisp little citrus cookies are our favorite all-purpose accompaniment to fruit desserts. Make up a batch of the dough and store it in the freezer as a hedge against entertaining emergencies—you'll be glad you did.

2 sticks (8 ounces) unsalted butter, softened
1½ cups sugar
2 tablespoons minced lemon zest
2 tablespoons minced lime zest
¼ teaspoon salt

4 egg yolks
3 tablespoons fresh lemon juice
3 tablespoons fresh lime juice
About 3 cups unbleached all-purpose flour

In a bowl, preferably of an electric stand mixer, cream together the butter, 1 cup of the sugar, the lemon and lime zests, and salt. One at a time beat in the egg yolks; stir in the lemon and lime juices. Add 2½ cups of the flour and mix until just combined. Transfer the dough to a container and chill it for at least 2 hours. *The dough can be prepared up to 3 days ahead and refrigerated or frozen for up to 1 month. Defrost the frozen dough in the refrigerator before using.*

Position racks in the upper and lower thirds of the oven and preheat the oven to 375°F. Grease several baking sheets.

Working in batches, by rounded tablespoonfuls, measure out the chilled dough and form it into 1-inch balls. Place the balls of dough on the baking sheets, spacing them well apart. Use the remaining flour to coat the flat bottom of a glass or measuring cup. Flatten the balls into 2-inch rounds about ¼-inch thick, reflouring the glass as necessary.

Bake the cookies, exchanging the position of the sheets on the racks from top to bottom and from front to back, for about 10 minutes or until the cookies are crisp and the edges and bottoms are lightly colored. With a spatula, transfer the cookies immediately to parchment paper and sprinkle them generously with the remaining ½ cup of sugar. *The cookies can be baked 1 day ahead and stored in an airtight container.*

makes about 4 dozen cookies

bizcochos

These traditional Mexican cookies must be made with lard to have the right consistency. We don't therefore eat them every day, but on special occasions, for special menus, there's nothing like a crisp-tender, spicy bizcocho. Cut them into different shapes for the kids, or just use a round cutter.

COOKIES
½ cup lard
¼ cup sugar
2 tablespoons sweet sherry, such as
   Harvey's Bristol Cream
2 tablespoons fresh orange juice

1 egg yolk
¾ cup unbleached all-purpose flour

COATING
½ cup sugar
½ teaspoon ground cinnamon
¼ teaspoon ground cloves

Position a rack in the upper and lower thirds of the oven and preheat the oven to 350°F.

In a mixer, whip the lard until it is light and creamy. Beat in the sugar, sherry, and orange juice. Beat in the egg yolk and then the flour.

Roll the dough out between layers of waxed paper to a thickness of ½ inch. Cut out cookies, transferring them to ungreased baking sheets. Bake them 12 to 15 minutes, exchanging the position of the sheets on the racks from top to bottom and from front to back at the halfway point, until the cookies are crisp and lightly colored.

For the coating, mix the sugar, cinnamon, and cloves in a wide shallow dish (like a pie plate). Carefully dredge the cookies in the spiced sugar while they are warm. Cool completely on a rack. Store at room temperature in airtight tins.

makes about 2 dozen

blueberry corn bread pudding with custard sauce

Smooth, sweet, and rich, this is our favorite bread pudding. It's good anytime but seems most appropriate on a brunch buffet. For convenience, as well as for the best texture, prepare the blueberry corn bread the day before you make the pudding.

5 eggs	1 recipe Blueberry Corn Bread (page
4 cups whipping cream	191), cut into 1-inch cubes
½ cup sugar	Custard Sauce (page 222)
2 teaspoons vanilla extract	Confectioners' sugar in a sieve

Position a rack in the middle of the oven and preheat the oven to 325°F. Butter a 9- by 13-inch baking pan.

In a large bowl, whisk the eggs thoroughly. Whisk in the cream, sugar, and vanilla extract. Add the corn bread cubes, stir once, just to coat the cubes with the custard, and then transfer the mixture to the baking pan. Distribute the cubes of bread and custard evenly in the pan and bake about 45 minutes, or until the pudding is puffed, the edges are lightly browned, and the pudding is evenly, but not firmly, set. Let the pudding stand on a rack until you serve it.

The pudding can be served warm or cool. Cut it into squares and place each square on a dessert plate. Spoon the sauce around each square, dust the tops of the squares lightly with confectioners' sugar, and serve immediately.

serves 9

custard sauce

4 egg yolks
¼ cup sugar
1⅓ cups half-and-half

¼ cup bourbon or 3 tablespoons
Triple Sec or other orange liqueur
½ teaspoon vanilla extract

In a medium bowl, whisk together the egg yolks and sugar. In a heavy saucepan, bring the half-and-half just to a simmer. Slowly whisk the hot half-and-half into the egg mixture. Return the mixture to the saucepan and set it over low heat. Cook, stirring constantly with a wooden spoon, until the mixture is thick enough to coat the back of the spoon and leaves a heavy track when a finger is drawn across it, about 4 minutes.

Transfer immediately to a bowl and stir in the bourbon or Triple Sec and vanilla extract. Cool completely, cover with plastic wrap, pressing the film onto the surface of the sauce, and refrigerate until cold, at least 5 hours. *The sauce can be prepared 3 days ahead.*

makes about 2¼ cups

sopaipillas

This recipe for the classic puffed fritters of the Southwest must be the best of its kind—nearly every cook we asked for advice gave it to us virtually word for word. We've even seen it in *Gourmet* magazine. We should point out that experience helps, and that failure of one or more of the sopaipillas to puff is not uncommon for beginners. They should be fried one at a time to give you control over both temperature and browning—there's nothing worse than a tough, overcooked sopaipilla. It's also worth serving them one at a time as they come fresh and hot out of the deep fat, in an assembly line of cooking and eating. They are drizzled with honey, of course (also good alongside a bowl of fiery chile verde—the honey helps with the heat), or they can be stuffed taco-like with a savory filling. Simply cut off a corner and spoon in well-fried beans or chili, plus cheese, lettuce, and salsa.

2 cups unbleached all-purpose flour
2½ teaspoons baking powder
½ teaspoon salt
2 tablespoons solid vegetable
   shortening

About ⅔ cup warm water
About 2 cups corn oil, for
   deep-frying
Honey

Sift together 1¾ cups of the flour, the baking powder, and salt. In a medium bowl, cut the shortening into the flour mixture. Gradually stir in the water until a loose dough is formed. Sprinkle 2 tablespoons of the remaining flour onto the work surface and knead about 1 minute, incorporating as much of the remaining flour as is required to make the dough manageable. Roll the dough out ¼-inch thick, cover it with a kitchen towel, and let it stand at least 15 minutes but not more than 30 minutes.

In a deep fryer or in a deep heavy pan fitted with a deep-fry thermometer, heat 2 inches of corn oil to between 375°F and 390°F. Trim the edges of the dough to form a neat rectangle. Cut the rectangle into twelve 3-inch triangle-shaped pieces. Lower one piece of dough into the oil, turn it immediately, and fry it, turning once more, until puffed and golden, about 1 minute. Transfer it to absorbent paper. Repeat this with the remaining dough. Serve hot, accompanied by honey.

For *Sospiras* ("Sighs"), cut the dough into 1½-inch squares. Fry several at a time, for between 30 and 45 seconds, or until puffed and golden. In a bowl, mix together ½ cup sugar and ½ teaspoon cinnamon. Toss the warm sospiras with the cinnamon-sugar until lightly coated. Serve immediately.
makes 12, serving 4 to 6

pineapple-apricot empanaditas

These ubiquitous little fruit-filled turnovers are an El Paso bakery passion. Usually made with a lard crust and frequently deep-fried as well, they're delicious but rich. Our version substitutes an easy, less rich, classic cream cheese pastry (from *James Beard's American Cookery*) for the lard-based one, and we prefer to bake our empanaditas. Canned pie fillings are commonly used (and some can be quite good), but for company we make our own fresh pineapple filling, flavor-boosted with apricot jam and Triple Sec. These empanaditas are great passed at a party, on a brunch buffet table, or at a picnic.

FILLING
1 large ripe pineapple
½ cup good-quality apricot
    preserves
3 tablespoons sugar
3 tablespoons Triple Sec
¼ cup fine dry (commercially pre-
    pared) bread crumbs

PASTRY
2 cups unbleached all-purpose flour
½ teaspoon salt
2 sticks (8 ounces) unsalted butter,
    slightly softened

6 ounces cream cheese, slightly
    softened

GLAZE
1 egg beaten with 1 tablespoon
    water
3 tablespoons sugar

∞∞∞∞∞∞∞∞∞∞∞∞

With a serrated knife, remove the top from the pineapple. Quarter the pineapple vertically and trim away the tough core from each quarter. Cut the pineapple flesh away from the rind. Chop the pineapple; there should be about 2¾ cups. In a medium saucepan, combine the pineapple, apricot jam, sugar, and Triple Sec. Set over medium heat and bring to a simmer. Cook, uncovered, stirring often, until thick, about 40 minutes. Cool to room temperature, and in a food processor partially purée the pineapple mixture. Some texture should remain. Stir in the bread crumbs. *The filling can be prepared up to 2 days ahead. Cover and refrigerate.*

In the work bowl of a food processor, combine the flour and salt and pulse briefly to blend. Add the butter and cream cheese and process until a soft dough forms.

Turn the dough out onto a lightly floured work surface and divide it in half. Gather each half into a ball, kneading briefly if necessary until smooth, and flatten each ball into a 5-inch disk. Wrap the disks of dough separately in plastic and refrigerate for at least 5 hours. *The dough can be prepared up to 2 days ahead.*

Let the disks of dough stand at room temperature until softened slightly. Dust one disc of dough with flour and on a well-floured surface roll it out to about ⅛-inch thick. Using a 3½-inch circular cutter, form the dough into about 12 rounds. Lay the rounds in a single layer on a plate or cookie sheet, wrap with plastic, and return them to the refrigerator. *Repeat with the remaining dough. The rounds of dough can be prepared 1 day ahead.*

Position racks in the upper and lower thirds of the oven and preheat the oven to 375°F. Lightly butter two large baking sheet pans.

Let the rounds of cream cheese pastry soften at room temperature just until flexible. Making one at a time, spread a heaping teaspoon of pineapple filling across the center of each round, leaving a border. Fold the round in half, then pinch the edges of the empanadita to seal and crimp it decoratively. Repeat with the remaining pastry rounds and filling, transferring the completed empanaditas to the baking sheets and spacing them well apart. Brush each empanadita with the egg wash and sprinkle it lightly with sugar. Bake the empanaditas, changing the position of the sheets on the racks from top to bottom and from front to back at the halfway point, until they are puffed, crisp, and golden, about 20 minutes. Cool them on a rack before serving. *The empanaditas can be prepared up to 1 day ahead and stored, airtight, at room temperature.*

makes about 24

crepes with cajeta and pecans

This easy, elegant dessert takes advantage of the rich caramel flavor of goat's milk–based cajeta (page 247). The golden cornmeal crepes can be prepared a day or two ahead, and need only to be rewarmed and garnished just before serving.

CREPES
1 cup half-and-half
2 eggs
2 teaspoons sugar
1 teaspoon vanilla extract
1 cup unbleached all-purpose flour
(measure by stirring with a fork, spooning into a dry measure, and sweeping level)
3 tablespoons yellow cornmeal, preferably stone-ground

2 tablespoons unsalted butter, melted
Corn oil, for the crepe pan

ASSEMBLY
½ cup pecans
4 tablespoons unsalted butter
1⅓ cups cajeta

FOR THE CREPES
In a blender or food processor, in the order listed, combine the half-and-half, eggs, sugar, vanilla extract, flour, cornmeal, and melted butter. Blend until smooth. Transfer to a bowl, cover, and let stand at room temperature for 1 hour.

Warm a 7-inch crepe pan, preferably nonstick, over medium-high heat. Brush it lightly with corn oil. Briefly stir the batter to recombine. When the pan is hot (the oil will smoke slightly), spoon ¼ cup batter into the skillet, tilting to coat the bottom completely. Set the pan over the heat, cook 20 seconds, turn the crepe, and cook another 10 seconds. Slide the crepe onto waxed paper. Repeat this with the remaining batter, stacking the crepes when cool between pieces of waxed paper. *The crepes can be wrapped tightly and refrigerated for up to 2 days.*

TO ASSEMBLE

Position a rack in the upper third of the oven and preheat the oven to 375°F.

Spread the pecans in a layer in a metal pan (like a cake tin) and toast them, stirring once or twice, until crisp and fragrant, 8 to 10 minutes. Remove them from the pan, cool, and coarsely chop them.

Fold the crepes in quarters, most attractive side out. Spread ½ tablespoon butter on the top of each crepe and wrap them in foil. Warm the crepes for about 15 minutes, or until they are hot and the butter has melted.

Meanwhile, in a small saucepan over low heat, warm the cajeta, stirring often. Arrange 2 crepes on each of 4 plates. Spoon the cajeta over and around them. Sprinkle the pecans over all and serve immediately.

serves 4

grilled pineapple with cajeta

A tart, juicy, perfectly ripe pineapple is not easily improved upon. One of the few credible ways to embellish this fragrant fruit is this intriguing warm dessert, which never fails to win us praise all out of proportion with its ease of preparation. The pineapple can be chunked and skewered, but we prefer to quarter it, grill the quarters, and then present them whole or sliced and fanned on the plate, in each case napped with warmed cajeta de leche—goat's milk–based sweet caramel sauce (page 247). If you grill over gas, which heats quickly, you can make this anytime. If you use charcoal, it will be more convenient to serve the pineapple after a grilled main course, cooked while the hot coals linger.

2 large juicy pineapples   2½ cups cajeta de leche
2 tablespoons corn oil

With a long serrated knife, cut off the tops and bottoms of the pineapple. Cut away the tough rind and quarter the pineapples vertically. Cut away the tough central core. *The pineapple quarters can be prepared several hours ahead. Wrap them well and refrigerate.*

Preheat a gas grill (medium) or light a charcoal fire and let it burn down until the coals are evenly white. Brush the pineapple with the corn oil. Set the rack about 6 inches above the heat source, lay the pineapple quarters on the grill rack, and cook, covered, adjusting the position of the pineapple on the grill to create attractive markings, for 4 minutes. Turn the pineapple quarters, cover, and grill another 4 minutes, again adjusting the position of the pineapple quarters on the rack, or until the pineapple is attractively marked and heated through.

Meanwhile, in a small saucepan over low heat, warm the cajeta, stirring often. Slice the pineapple, fan the slices on dessert plates, and generously nap with the warm caramel sauce. Serve immediately.

serves 8

a hot smoky night

Chilled White Wine

Chipotle Salsa del Norte (page 4) with Tostaditas (page 32)
Queso Fundido on the Grill (page 20) with Soft Corn Tortillas

Grilled Tuna with Orange-Chili Marinade (page 88)
Grilled Vegetable Platter (page 186)
Texas Toast (page 189)

Grilled Pineapple with Cajeta (page 228)
Lemon-Lime Cookies (page 219)

mango-peach ice cream with dulce crunch

Mangoes and peaches taste so good together they give credence to the theory that foods of approximately the same color are always successful flavor partners. In this ice cream, Amaretto joins vanilla extract, and the finished dessert is topped, if desired, with crunchy chopped candied pecans.

4 cups whipping cream
3 cups half-and-half
8 egg yolks
1½ cups sugar
1½ teaspoons vanilla extract
2 pounds very ripe peaches

4 very ripe medium mangoes
¼ cup Amaretto
2 tablespoons fresh lemon juice
2 cups coarsely chopped Dulces
  (candied pecans, page 235)

In a large heavy saucepan over medium heat, combine the whipping cream and half-and-half. Bring the mixture just to a boil.

Meanwhile, in a large bowl, whisk the egg yolks. Whisk in 1 cup of the sugar. Slowly dribble the hot cream into the egg mixture, whisking constantly. Return this mixture to the pan, set it over low heat, and cook, stirring constantly with a wooden spoon, until the mixture thickens sufficiently to heavily coat the back of the spoon and leaves a track when a finger is drawn across it, 4 to 5 minutes. Do not allow the mixture to boil. Transfer this custard to a large bowl, stir in the vanilla extract, and cool to room temperature.

Bring a medium pan of water to a boil. One or two at a time, lower the peaches into the water, wait 30 seconds, then with a slotted spoon, transfer the peaches to a large bowl of cold water. Peel the peaches (the skins will slip off easily) and pit them. In a large bowl, coarsely mash them.

Peel and pit the mangoes and in a food processor, purée the flesh. Combine the mango purée with the mashed peaches, the remaining ½ cup of sugar, Amaretto, and lemon juice. Stir in the cooled custard mixture. Cover with plastic wrap, pressing the film onto the surface of the custard, and refrigerate until very cold, preferably overnight.

In the canister of an ice-cream maker, churn the ice cream according to the manufacturer's directions. Cover the finished ice cream and store it in the freezer. If necessary, allow it to soften slightly in the refrigerator before scooping. Sprinkle each portion with chopped dulces, if desired, and serve immediately.

makes about 1 gallon

kahlúa chocolate sauce

This intense and elegant coffee-chocolate sauce keeps for weeks in the refrigerator and reheats perfectly in a microwave oven. It's wonderful on ice cream and as a dip for strawberries and is indispensable drizzled around and over a slice of Adobe Pie (page 215).

1½ sticks (6 ounces) unsalted butter
6 ounces semisweet chocolate, chopped
¾ cup plus 2 tablespoons sugar
¾ cup lightly packed Dutch process cocoa powder

1½ teaspoons powdered instant espresso
½ cup corn syrup
¾ cup whipping cream
½ cup Kahlúa
1 teaspoon vanilla extract

In a medium-size heavy saucepan over low heat, melt the butter and chocolate together, stirring occasionally, until smooth.

Whisk in the sugar. Sift in the cocoa powder, whisking as you do. Add the espresso and corn syrup. Slowly whisk in the cream and Kahlúa. Bring just to a boil, stirring often. Lower the heat and simmer for 5 minutes, stirring once or twice and scraping down the sides of the pan with a rubber spatula.

Remove the sauce from the heat. Stir in the vanilla extract and transfer the sauce immediately to a heat-proof container with a lid. Cool completely, cover, and store in the refrigerator. The sauce should sit at least 24 hours to mellow the flavor and texture.

To serve, remove the desired amount from the container and warm it in a double boiler or in a microwave oven, stirring, until hot.

makes 1 quart

norma's quick and easy frozen mango dessert

Though this dessert is quickly assembled from canned fruits, it has an icy freshness that is particularly welcome after a rich and fiery Southwestern entrée.

1 28-ounce can sliced mangoes in heavy syrup
2 14-ounce cans apricot halves in heavy syrup

16 maraschino cherries, drained and patted dry or 16 whole fresh raspberries
Unsweetened whipped cream, for garnish (optional)

Pour the mangoes and their syrup into a 9- by 13-inch dish. Drain the apricot halves, reserving the syrup. Arrange the apricot halves among the mango slices, pitted-sides up. Randomly place the maraschino cherries in the concave spots in some of the apricot halves. Shake the dish to cover the apricot halves and cherries with the mango syrup. If they are not covered, drizzle additional apricot syrup over them. Cover the dish and place it in the freezer until the dessert is solid, at least 5 hours. *This dessert can be prepared up to 3 days ahead. Let it soften slightly in the refrigerator before serving. The texture should be icy but not hard.*

To serve it, cut it into rectangles, transfer them to chilled dessert plates, and garnish, if desired, with whipped cream. Serve immediately.

serves 8

pear and cactus pear ice

Tunas—or cactus pears—are the deep red fruit of the prickly pear cactus. They're found in many markets around the country, though on an irregular basis, and interested cooks will have to keep an eye out for these egg-shaped curiosities. We're lucky enough to find them for sale from street vendors in Juárez (usually in late summer), already peeled, which saves us doing that thorny job at home. Full of seeds and light on flavor (think of strawberry diluted by watermelon), they nevertheless produce an astonishingly crimson juice that we combine with ripe pear purée to create this cooling dessert. Serve it as is, or on top of slices of ripe mango, and drizzle each scoop of ice, if you like, with a tablespoon of gold tequila.

2½ pounds (about 10 large) prickly
    pear tunas
2 pounds (about 4 large) very ripe
    Bartlett pears, peeled, cored, and
    chunked

1 cup sugar
¼ cup fresh lime juice
2 tablespoons Triple Sec or other
    orange liqueur

Trim both ends from each prickly pear tuna and cut away the thick peel. (Some tunas are pricklier than others, and you may wish to impale the tunas on a fork to protect your fingers while peeling.) Cut the fruit into small chunks.

In a food processor, purée the chunks of tuna. Transfer the purée to a strainer set over a bowl. With a rubber scraper, force the purée and juice through the strainer; discard the seeds.

In the food processor (wipe the work bowl free of seeds but there is no need to clean it), purée together the pear chunks, sugar, lime juice, and Triple Sec. Combine the pear purée with the prickly pear purée and chill, covered, until very cold, at least 5 hours and preferably overnight.

Transfer the chilled fruit mixture to the canister of an ice-cream maker and churn according to the manufacturer's directions. Store the finished ice, covered, in the freezer, softening it slightly in the refrigerator if necessary before serving.

makes about 2 quarts

forti's almond flan

At Forti's Mexican Elder, one of El Paso's best restaurants, the almond flan is delicious. Consuelo Forti and her daughter Gina have worked with night chef Angela Garcia to translate their restaurant-size recipe into one suitable for home cooks.

¾ cup sugar
8 eggs
5 cups milk
1 can (12 ounces) sweetened
   condensed milk

5 tablespoons vanilla extract
2½ tablespoons almond extract
1 teaspoon ground cinnamon

In a small heavy saucepan, set the sugar over low heat. Cook, stirring often, until the sugar melts and turns a rich amber. Working quickly, coat the sides and bottoms of eight 6-ounce dessert dishes, one at a time, with the caramel.

Position a rack in the middle of the oven and preheat the oven to 350°F.

Using a stand mixer, beat the eggs until thick. Beat in the milk, sweetened condensed milk, vanilla extract, almond extract, and cinnamon and continue to beat until the mixture is light and frothy. Divide the milk mixture among the caramel-lined dishes and set the dishes into a large baking pan. Add hot tap water to the baking pan to come halfway up the sides of the dishes and bake until the custards are evenly set but not firm, about 45 minutes. Remove from the water bath, cool to room temperature, and refrigerate for at least 1 hour. *The flans can be prepared up to 3 days ahead. Cover them with plastic and keep refrigerated.*

To serve, run a sharp knife around the inside edge of each dish. Cover the dish with a plate and invert the plate and dish together; the flan and its caramel syrup will drop out onto the plate. Serve immediately, or put the plates of flan in the refrigerator until serving time.

serves 8

dulces
(*candied pecans*)

We manufacture a version of this traditional Mexican candy and having it on hand enables us to use it in all sorts of ways, including chopped as a topping sprinkled over ice cream (particularly Mango-Peach Ice Cream, page 230). It's also good as a nibble with coffee, or anytime you get a craving for a crunchy, pralinelike candy. This recipe, which is quite close to the one we make, is adapted from *El Norte* by James W. Peyton, the best work by far we have seen on the foods of northern Mexico. Making it, however, is not very successful during humid weather.

2 cups half-and-half	2 tablespoons vanilla extract
2 cups packed light brown sugar	2 tablespoons dark rum
¼ cup light corn syrup	2 cups (about 8 ounces) pecans

Lightly butter a jelly roll pan.

In a medium heavy saucepan over moderate heat, combine the half-and-half, light brown sugar, corn syrup, vanilla extract, and rum. Stir until melted. Bring to a boil, stir in the pecans, and cook at a full boil until a candy thermometer registers 260°F and a spoonful dropped onto the baking sheet firmly holds its shape.

Immediately drop heaping tablespoonfuls of the pecan mixture onto the prepared sheet. Cool to room temperature and store in an airtight tin.

makes about 1 pound

chapter thirteen

quenchers
drinks to douse the fire

Chill out. That's our advice. When the day's a scorcher or when your lunch sets your lips on fire, turn to one of the long, tall, mostly cool beverages in the following chapter. Hospitality in west Texas can be as simple as a glass of ice water but usually extends to something with a little more octane in it. Our quenchers here are not numerous and you don't have to stick just with them—be adaptive and creative (when in Houston, we drink martinis like everyone else), but they're tasty, they do the trick, and they'll get you started.

the classic 1-1-1 margarita

This drink has the potent intensity of a gimlet and recalls the more elegant, grown-up era of cocktails, before margaritas came in pitchers or were frozen like sorbets. Made with slightly sweeter Mexican limes, this margarita is perfect; if you use the tarter Persian limes found in the United States, it may require the addition of a pinch of sugar.

Ice
3 tablespoons gold tequila

3 tablespoons orange liqueur
3 tablespoons fresh lime juice

In a cocktail shaker filled with ice, combine the tequila, orange liqueur, and lime juice. Shake until cold and strain into a wide salt-rimmed martini glass. Serve immediately.

makes 1 cocktail

classic tequila sunrise

Because of the orange juice it contains and because of its pastel colors, the tequila sunrise seems to us to be the perfect brunch drink (even though that means enjoying it closer to sunrise than sunset). For the best results, use gold tequila and fresh orange juice (or a combination of fresh orange and pink grapefruit juices). A splash of club soda will lighten things up.

Ice
½ cup fresh orange juice
3 tablespoons gold tequila

1 teaspoon grenadine syrup
Splash of club soda (optional)
Wedge of fresh lime

In a tall glass filled with ice, stir together the orange juice and tequila. Pour the grenadine into the cocktail, letting it sink to the bottom. Add club soda if you want, squeeze the lime into the drink, and serve immediately.

makes 1 cocktail

park's easy frozen margaritas

Ready in minutes, these are breathtakingly cold and slushy, and if you have previously not enjoyed frozen margaritas, they may well change your mind. Controy Licor de Naranjas, an orange-flavored Mexican liqueur, is Park's preference for these, but Triple Sec may be substituted.

1 6-ounce container frozen limeade
   concentrate, defrosted
1½ cups gold tequila
¾ cup orange liqueur

4 trays of ice cubes
1 6-ounce container frozen pineapple juice concentrate, defrosted
3 medium limes, quartered

In a blender, combine the limeade concentrate, half the tequila, and half the orange liqueur. Fill the blender almost to the top with ice. Blend on high speed until thick and slushy. Transfer to a pitcher. In the blender, combine the remaining tequila, remaining orange liqueur, and pineapple juice concentrate. Fill the blender almost to the top with ice and blend on high speed until thick and slushy. Transfer to the pitcher and stir to combine. Serve the margaritas immediately, using salt-rimmed glasses if desired, and squeezing fresh lime juice onto the top of each drink.

makes 12 generous cocktails

three-alarm bloody marys

We use our Snakebite Salsa in these eye-opening Bloody Marys, since the puréed red chiles with which the salsa is prepared add an extra depth of flavor. Any really spicy tomato-based salsa can be substituted, though, as long as it is puréed before being mixed with the other ingredients. For Bloody Marias, substitute gold tequila for the vodka and serve the cocktails in salt-rimmed glasses. The amount of liquor you use is up to you—two cups will produce a medium-strength drink.

1½ cups tomato-based bottled
   hot salsa
1 46-ounce can tomato juice
3 tablespoons fresh lime juice

2 tablespoons Worcestershire sauce
About 2 cups lemon vodka
Wedges of fresh lime, for garnish

In a food processor, purée the salsa until smooth. In a large pitcher, stir together the puréed salsa, tomato juice, lime juice, Worcestershire sauce, and lemon vodka to taste. Cover and refrigerate until very cold, preferably overnight.

Stir to blend and serve the Bloody Marys over ice, garnished with a wedge of lime.

makes 8 generous cocktails

white sangria

This tall cool drink is not only delicious but pretty, and it makes a nice change from beer or margaritas. We make it with peaches, but plums, nectarines, sweet cherries, and raspberries can also be used.

1½ liters dry white wine
½ cup orange liqueur
2 pounds ripe peaches, washed,
   pitted, and sliced
1 lemon, thinly sliced

1 lime, thinly sliced
Ice
Club soda
Additional fresh fruit, for garnish
   (optional)

In a large jar or pitcher, stir together the white wine and orange liqueur. Stir in the peaches and lemon and lime slices, and refrigerate, covered, for at least 3 days and up to 1 week.

Strain the sangria, discarding the fruit. Pour it over ice in tall glasses and add a splash of soda. Garnish with fresh fruit, if desired, and serve immediately.

serves 8

rio grande lemonade

If you've forgotten how good genuine fresh lemonade tastes, drink this on a hot and dusty El Paso summer's day! We serve it over lots of ice in 1-pint glass canning jars (Kerr brand, if we can, for the monogrammed look) and find it equally tasty made with good bourbon. To make pink lemonade for the kids and other teetotalers, replace the alcohol with an equal quantity of bottled cranberry juice.

5 cups fresh lemon juice (from
    about 24 large lemons)
3½ cups water

1½ cups gold tequila
3 cups sugar, or to taste

In a gallon jar, combine the lemon juice, water, tequila, and 2½ cups of the sugar. Stir well, cover, and refrigerate until very cold, preferably overnight.

Stir well, adjust the seasoning, and serve the lemonade over ice.

serves 10 to 12

whipped mexican chocolate

Traditionally Mexican chocolate is whipped up with a wooden pestlelike implement called a *molinillo,* although nowadays a more modern device, the *liquadora* ("blender"), does the hard work.

Half a 3.1-ounce tablet of Mexican
    chocolate, preferably Ibarra
    brand, finely chopped

1 cup milk
½ cup whipping cream

Place the chopped chocolate in a blender. In a small saucepan over medium heat, combine the milk and whipping cream and bring to a full boil. Immediately pour the hot milk mixture over the chocolate in the blender. Cover and process on high speed until smooth and frothy. Pour into 2 mugs and serve immediately.

makes 2 servings

norma's iced mango tea with mint

It is obvious that Norma loves mangoes, and when she discovered mango-flavored tea, it took her no time at all to realize its possibilities. A tall glass of iced tea is an automatic Texas welcome (restaurant waiters are more likely to set a glass of iced tea, unordered, in front of a patron than a glass of iced water). A frosty pitcher of this beverage, garnished with fresh mint, is a daily cooler at Norma's house during the summer and for much of the rest of the year as well.

1 gallon water
8 tablespoons mango-flavored tea
4 tablespoons orange pekoe tea

Sprigs of fresh mint, for garnish (optional)

In a saucepan over medium heat, bring 1 quart of the water to a boil. Stir in the mango and orange pekoe teas and let stand, off the heat, covered, for 5 minutes.

Strain the tea into a large jar or pitcher, discarding the leaves. Add 3 quarts of warm water and cool to room temperature. Serve the tea over ice in tall glasses, garnished with a sprig of mint if desired.

makes 1 gallon

iced kahlúa coffee

Strong iced coffee and the unique Mexican liqueur Kahlúa are combined in this dessert cocktail, perfect with cookies and fresh fruit on a hot summer's day. We use ice cubes of the same coffee frozen one day ahead—plain ice dilutes the drink.

Ice cubes of frozen coffee (optional)
3 tablespoons Kahlúa

½ cup strong-brewed coffee, prefer-ably at least 50 percent dark roast, at room temperature
1 tablespoon whipping cream

Fill a tall glass with cubes of frozen coffee or with regular ice cubes. Pour the Kahlúa over the ice. Pour the coffee over the ice. Float the cream on top of the coffee and serve with a long spoon.

makes 1 cocktail

ingredients of the el paso pantry

Not everything cooked everyday in El Paso is totally authentic (whatever that misused word means), but we are influenced by our surroundings in hundreds of subtle ways. Just knowing one can find ripe tomatoes, fresh cilantro, and good avocados daily at the market means we cook a whole different way from, say, people living in Boston or Seattle. The basics are discussed in this section, and while we've been scrupulously honest about those substitutions that work and those that don't, the bad news is, for true regional flavor, it is necessary to use some regional ingredients. The good news is, many of these ingredients are increasingly available, not only in gourmet food stores but in supermarkets as well. The country's increasing Hispanic population, in addition to the growing interest in Southwestern cooking, means stocking your El Paso pantry is easier than ever. (And, when all else fails, turn to the Appendix on page 259 where we give mail-order sources for authentic ingredients).

avocados

You'll see two kinds in the market. One, from Florida, is huge, bright green, and nearly always too bland, stringy, and wet to be of much use. The other, widely grown in California and aggressively marketed by an avocado cooperative, is pear-shaped and smaller, and when it's ripe, the bumpy skin is a glossy black. The several related varieties are usually lumped together under the name of the best-known, Hass. The pale-green-to-yellow flesh has more flavor, more fat, and more calories, which is why it is so seductive. Avocados, once ripe, quickly become rank and inedible, and since greengrocers would rather that happens on your kitchen counter than in their shop, they are usually found three to five days short of perfection, rendering guacamole and other avocado-based preparations unsuitable for spontaneous cooking. Plan ahead, letting the avocados ripen at home at room temperature, then use them immediately once they're ripe (just softly yielding to gentle thumb pressure), without refrigeration.

beans

Beans are one of the great staples of the Southwest, providing not only nutrition (in a land where animal protein was originally scarce) but great eating as well. Beans are earthy-tasting but otherwise neutral, and they welcome zesty Southwestern seasonings. Pinto beans are seen most often around El Paso, followed distantly by black beans, garbanzo beans, black-eyed peas, and kidney beans. Dried beans are affordable and keep virtually forever; canned beans are a convenience, though brands vary widely in quality—look for those that remain firm and fresh-tasting after the packing liquid is rinsed off. Soaking dried beans in several changes of water for twenty-hour hours or so removes some of the ingredients that cause gas, and also lets the beans cook more quickly and evenly, but some of the most authentic bean preparations call for unsoaked beans that are cooked until they fall apart. The technique of quick soaking can be used if time is short: Cover unsoaked beans with cold water, bring it to a full boil, then cool them to room temperature in the water. Drain them, add fresh water, and again bring it to a boil; the beans will now cook in about the same time as if they had been soaked overnight.

cajeta de leche

This thick, caramely syrup, based on goat's milk, is a unique Mexican confection. Originally named for the boxes (or *cajas*) into which it was poured after cooking, the delicious stuff comes in everything from rustic pottery crocks to factory-packed jars. Cow's milk versions are also seen nowadays, but we prefer the tangy edge goat's milk gives to the cajeta. Our pantry is never without a jar or two, and all it takes is warming it slightly over low heat or in the microwave oven to give us a sweet, golden sauce to pour over pecan-dotted crepes (page 226), grilled pineapple (page 228), ice cream, pound cake, waffles, etc., etc.

cheeses

Mexican border cheeses are, in general, mild and somewhat bland, occasionally slightly acidic, fresher and milky-tasting rather than aged and sharp. *Asadero,* often sold in stacks of thin round sheets called tortillas, is sometimes made with *trompillas,* small wild berries that cause milk to coagulate just as animal rennet does. Chihuahua, also called *queso menenito* or Mennonite cheese, was first produced by Mennonite farmers who founded an agricultural community in central Chihuahua. Now produced by other cheese makers as well, it is sold in wedges cut from large wheels. Both cheeses melt easily and string attractively—qualities much sought after by Mexicans, and while some El Paso cheese makers (such as Lincon Dairy) make excellent cheeses, we often cross the border to shop at the Cuauhtemoc Market in Juárez. On the U.S. side, less successful American versions of both cheeses can be found in supermarkets, and cooks here have learned to substitute Monterey Jack or mozzarella (or a combination of the two) and medium-sharp cheddar. Feta cheese is often substituted for queso anejo, a sharper dried cheese that does not melt. Though not very traditional, tangy fresh goat cheeses have a wonderful affinity for border food, and we don't hesitate to experiment with them.

chicharrones

Great curled sheets of deep-fried pork skin are a popular local snack. George Bush did much to tip off the rest of the country to the seductively crunchy qualities of chicharrones, but in El Paso we've enjoyed this treat for many years. Chicharrones can be simmered into fillings or sauces, but we like them best broken into small pieces and dipped into guacamole or hot salsas, just as we use tostaditas.

chiles—fresh, frozen, dried, and canned

Nothing says more about the spreading acceptance of Southwestern food than the growing interest in chiles of all kinds. America can't seem to get enough of the hot stuff, a state of affairs that makes us very happy indeed. El Pasoans in particular like things fiery (practice and training have a lot to do with chile tolerance), though in our recipes we have tried to give a range in order to accommodate palates that are just getting into shape. It is also worth knowing that stresses of weather, soil, and other imponderables can cause wild fluctuations in the heat level of almost any chile type—such unpredictability being part of the general excitement of cooking with these fiery fruits. Whatever the heat level, chiles come fresh, frozen, dried, or in cans or jars, and each form requires different techniques and has different uses.

The Southwestern United States (as opposed to Mexico proper) cooks with a fairly limited larder of chiles. Fresh chiles are perishable and will turn up only where grocers can be certain of selling them fairly quickly. Among them the small, fat, bright green jalapeños are the most widely available. Hot to very hot, they are good raw or cooked and can be flame-roasted ("parched" as local cooks say) to remove the peel and add a smoky richness. Fresh jalapeños (and all fresh chiles) should be stored unwashed and loosely wrapped in the vegetable keeper of your refrigerator.

Yellow wax or banana peppers (*chiles güero*) are slightly larger than jalapeños and at about the same heat level, and local cooks use them interchangeably, especially in the chunky raw salsa called Pico de Gallo (page 3).

Serranos are smaller and hotter than jalapeños, with an excellent flavor. When we find them in El Paso (and not all that often), we substitute about one and a half serranos for each jalapeño called for.

Poblanos, dark green, wedge-shaped chiles, ranging from medium to large and from sweetly *picante* to fairly fiery, are among the most complex-tasting and highly regarded chiles in Mexico. We see them occasionally in El Paso markets and use them fire-roasted, stemmed, seeded, and cut into ¼-inch-long strips (*rajas*) that can be used as an ingredient without further embellishment, or marinated with a little olive oil and crushed garlic and used as a garnish in any number of dishes. Though we usually make chiles rellenos with long green chiles, in Mexico poblanos would be used, and they make magnificent rellenos.

"Long green" is the generic expression we have used in this book for a type of chile pod commonly called anaheim. In El Paso using that name can get your butt kicked, since we don't think a town whose main claim to fame is Disneyland has any business symbolizing a crop we grow better and more abundantly than anywhere else on the planet. Actually, though there is a local chile crop, most of the growing goes on north of here, in New Mexico's Mesilla Valley (the little town of Hatch is virtually the chile-growing capital of the country and the site of an annual chile festival), and even Texans admit that New Mexico's green chiles are superior to all others. They are cousins of the anaheim, but several (Big Jim and New Mexico No. 6–4, for example) have been improved, crossbred, and otherwise genetically tinkered with (sort of like corn has been in Iowa) to maximize commercial potential. Since they are the major cash crop of New Mexico, as well as the source of plenty of good eating, the effort is clearly worth it.

The seasonal harvest begins to show up around Labor Day (in supermarket aisles stacks of boxes of Velveeta and bins of long green chiles announce the local passion for chile con queso and chiles rellenos) and remains more or less constant until frost sets in. Fresh long green New Mexico chiles are available, in season, from a number of mail-order sources.

For most uses, long green chiles must be roasted, preferably in an open flame, to remove the tough peel and partially cook the flesh. With the beginning of the chile harvest, propane-fired rotary chile roasters show up in supermarket parking lots, and savvy cooks stock up on gunny sacks of long greens while the prices are low. (Purists patiently parch their chiles a few at a time at home, often on a grill over mesquite wood chips, but the convenience of bulk roasting can't be denied. There are also proponents of parching by immersion in deep fat. This may be convenient for restaurants with banks of Fry-O-Lators at the ready, but we find it messy and unpleasant work.)

If you have roasted red peppers for Italian and French preparations, you will be familiar with the general technique. With the tip of a knife, a small steam vent is poked in the stem end of chiles to be used whole, to prevent bursting. In the open flame of a gas burner, or under a preheated electric broiler (less successful), the chiles are turned often until the skin is blistered and lightly charred. The chiles are steamed until cool in a closed paper bag or on a plate covered with a bowl.

For immediate use of the chiles, the burned peel is rubbed off and the chiles are cut into rajas or slit partially open and gently deseeded with a fingertip, to be stuffed and served whole. Charred but otherwise left whole and unpeeled, the chiles can be bagged in plastic and frozen for a year's worth of great eating. When needed they are defrosted and peeled, and even in such chile-centric preparations as chiles rellenos they are excellent. Fresh long greens from elsewhere (even, we suppose, Anaheim) can be had at premium prices at other times of the year, for those who crave rellenos and have neglected to stock their freezers.

Frozen whole and chopped, roasted green chiles are also sold commercially, packed in containers ranging from small tubs to five-pound bags, and can be ordered by mail. Of canned green chiles, however—the sort available in most American supermarkets—there is not much except convenience to be said. Usually steamed rather than roasted, they are mere shadows of the real thing.

Near the end of the season the long green chiles ripen on the plant to bright red, when they are at their most perishable, and, maddeningly, at their sweet, hot best. These don't travel well, but we make the most of them while they last, and those that don't get eaten or frozen get dried, to be turned into long ornamental strings (*ristras*) or sold loose in bulk. Dried long red chiles are soaked to be reconstituted and softened, then they are puréed and sieved, to remove any remaining seeds and hard bits of peel. This is the best way for those who live elsewhere than chile country to savor the taste of red New Mexico chiles, and to this end frozen and jarred versions of red chile paste are also marketed and available by mail order. Long red chiles are also ground into powder and cooks can capture much of the same flavor by seeking out a good, fresh product. The Chimayo area, northeast of Santa Fe, produces what is accepted as the finest chiles for chili powder, and when available it is proudly labeled as such.

Aside from the dried long red chiles with which most local cooks content themselves, a few other dried chiles are occasionally used, usually by cooks with strong ties to Mexico or by adventurers in the new Southwestern cuisine. Dried poblanos are called anchos and have a rich, deep, almost chocolaty flavor and a perfectly balanced heat that make them a fine addition to more complex sauces. Dried chipotles (smoked jalapeños) are occasionally used in such long-simmered preparations as Caldo Tla-peno (page 108), but they are difficult to soften enough to purée into most dishes. For a hot accent (when your dried red chile pods are on the mild side), add a few chiles de arbol or japones or chiltepins to the purée or to a simmering pot. Two or three of any of these small-to-tiny dried red chiles will rapidly raise the heat level of whatever dish uses them.

Most canned chiles, as we have mentioned, have few uses, although there are two exceptions. Pickled jalapeños (*en escabeche*) retain their crunchy texture and fire and acquire a tart tang that is delicious. Canned chipotles, packed in a vinegary tomato-based sauce (abodo), are brick-red, smoky, and quite addicting (also very hot) and we use them as a seasoning in many sauces or dishes and straight from the can as a condiment. Both pickled jalapeños and chipotles adobado (the latter transferred out of their cans to a glass or plastic container) will keep for a month or longer in the refrigerator.

chili powder blend

Chili powder blend is a widely available prepared seasoning mix consisting of one or more kinds of ground red chiles, along with such seasonings as paprika, oregano, cumin, and garlic salt, designed to make the preparation of chili con carne easier and more predictable. We manufacture a chili powder blend and use it increasingly in dishes where a convenient, well-rounded, Southwestern flavor is wanted. The best blends are not too hot, allowing those who like their Southwestern fare flavorful but mild to use the full amount of chili powder blend called for. (Cutting back won't make a dish less spicy—only less tasty.) Jalapeños, cayenne pepper, crushed red pepper, bottled hot sauce or salsa provide additional fire where wanted, and hot heads know this can be added to the pot by the cook at the stove, or to each bowl by the diner at the table.

chocolate

It is understandable, since the use of chocolate originated in ancient Mexico, that much is still made of it there today. Mexican chocolate, or the kind we find the most useful anyway, comes flavored with ground almonds, cinnamon, and vanilla. It makes delicious hot chocolate (page 242), but we continually explore new ways of substituting it for ordinary sweetened chocolate in traditional America recipes. It can sometimes be replaced with ordinary sweetened chocolate, augmented with ground cinnamon, extra vanilla and almond extracts to taste, but Ibarra brand—one of the best—is widely available by mail order and is found in some gourmet shops. It comes in hexagonal or octagonal disks or tablets, packaged in several weights. The probability of finding the exact size tablet in the market needed for any given recipe is low, and we usually buy whatever we find and weigh the chocolate, at cooking time, on a kitchen scale.

chorizo

This highly seasoned pork sausage is found in supermarkets and is most useful in bulk form. (The chorizo of El Paso is not the dry-cured, firm link sausage found in Spanish markets.) The texture is fine and rather loose (there is a lot of water in the mix), and it is always precooked to render out fat and moisture. To do this, the meat is crumbled in a skillet and sautéed over low heat, stirred often, until lightly browned, about 15 minutes. The cooked chorizo is transferred to absorbent paper to drain. We find it easier to cook a pound or more at a time and then freeze the meat in small amounts, to be defrosted whenever we want it for use in quesadillas, breakfast burritos, and so on.

cilantro

You either love or hate this pungent herb (also known as fresh coriander and Chinese parsley), but its popularity these days is such that you certainly won't be able to avoid it. (We remember well the outrage of a friend, less than fond of cilantro, who found her otherwise impeccable restaurant order of cheese tortellini generously seasoned with the stuff.) For true appreciation, try an extended visit to Mexico, where cilantro's pungent quality seems the very soul of cookery. It is another perishable ingredient that can be difficult to locate. The fragile leaves should be unwilted (the herb is usually sold in bunches with the roots left on) and stored in the refrigerator upright in a jar of water, like cut flowers. Drape a plastic bag over the bouquet for extra protection and plan to use the cilantro within a couple of days. Some dishes will call for just the leaves, chopped, while others in which the cilantro is puréed can include the stems.

corn

It can hardly be said too often that corn is the great staple of Southwestern cooking. With beans providing protein balance and chiles adding the savory emphasis, the bare bones of this great cuisine are revealed and completed. Corn is used in several forms.

Mainly the corn staples we eat are produced from tough field corn (though sugary, tender ears of sweet corn are also increasingly enjoyed). Dried, these corn kernels are called chicos. Slaked in a strong solution of lime and water, the chicos' tough outer skins are loosened and the corn acquires a distinctive flavor. These treated kernels are called posole and can be simmered into soups and stews or to be eaten whole. Posole can be purchased in this form in bags in supermarkets and ordered by mail. Posole that is fully husked and cooked until tender is called hominy and can be purchased canned, packed in water, for use as an easy starch for soups, stews, and side dishes. There is both white and yellow hominy—and we discern no flavor difference.

Slaked corn kernels are also ground into the moist, mealy dough—masa—that is used in fresh corn tortillas, gorditas, tamales, and tamale pie. It is considered that tamales and tortillas made from fresh masa are superior, but there is also a dried treated cornmeal—masa harina de maiz—that can be used as an acceptable alternative. Quaker is the most commonly seen brand, and we have used it in preparations calling for masa in this book with good results. (Fine- or coarse-grain masa can be used interchangeably in our recipes.) Good-quality fresh masa can also be purchased by mail and stored in the freezer until use.

Ordinary American cornmeal is also an El Paso staple, without which we couldn't make corn bread, corn waffles, corn crepes, and so on—not to mention polenta, although that is probably another book! Stone-ground cornmeal retains the germ, and while it is more perishable, it has a fuller corn flavor. Buy small amounts and store the meal in the refrigerator or freezer to extend its shelf life.

Preferences for white or yellow cornmeal are regional; we have noticed no flavor difference. Generally, since the golden color is more attractive and more "corny" we cook with yellow meal.

Except, of course, when we cook with blue cornmeal. You may be tired of hearing about this Southwestern staple, but don't dismiss it as trendy; Indians have been grinding and cooking with the indigenous blue corn almost as long as there has been cultivation in the Americas.

Not truly blue (more a purple-gray), the corn is not easy to grow, must be hand-cultivated, is more perishable—and yet for all that is gaining popularity for one simple reason: It tastes great. The meal is tricky to make into tortillas (we don't try, preferring to order ours by mail), but it can be used in corn bread and corn cake recipes, and packaged blue corn tostaditas are increasingly available. The dramatic color is just right in Southwestern cookery, and the intense corn flavor, essential.

Sweet corn has been hybridized to retain its tenderness and natural sugars, and the old advice that the water should be boiling before the corn is even picked is no longer sound. Such supersweet hybrids as Kandy Korn and Honey and Cream are sweet days after picking and need only a few minutes of simmering in water or a quick turn over hot coals to be ready to eat, anointed with butter, lime juice, and a generous shake of chili powder.

crema

Crema is cultured heavy cream, made exactly the same way crème fraîche is, if you are familiar with that thick, tart, rich French delight. To make it, combine 2 cups heavy cream (preferably *not* ultra-pasteurized) with 2 or 3 tablespoons cultured buttermilk or plain yogurt and let stand, loosely covered, at room temperature for 12 hours. The cream will thicken and become acidic. Cover it and refrigerate until you use it; the crema will thicken further and will keep for up to 10 days. Unlike sour cream, crema can be boiled, and unlike sour cream, crema softens and runs into luxurious puddles atop such dishes as Enchiladas de las Colonias (page 36), where we deem it to be essential to the enjoyment of the dish. Those with a good cheese department or cheese store can purchase imported crème fraîche if desired.

cumin

Tex-Mex fever has increased the use of this spice manyfold over the last ten years, and for many if it isn't heavily dosed with cumin it doesn't taste authentic. Mexicans don't apply cumin with the same gusto Americans do, and in El Paso we don't use as much of it as folks in central Texas. Still, it's a staple spice we wouldn't want to cook without. For a nuttier, richer flavor, toast the seeds, stirring them over low heat in a small heavy ungreased skillet for about 7 minutes, or until they are a rich brown. Toast a quantity (small amounts tend to scorch), store them in a tightly covered jar, and grind them with a mortar and pestle or in a spice mill just before you use them.

epazote

This pungent herb is hardly essential to El Paso cooking, but since planting it in our garden, where it is gradually assuming control of all living things, we are growing increasingly fond of epazote. Also called goosefoot or wormseed, it has a fragrance and flavor that experts describe as camphorlike, although to us it smells more like turpentine. Such industrial-strength hairsplitting aside, epazote adds an ineffable something to black Frijoles de Olla (page 178), and we love it sprinkled onto quesadillas of rajas of poblano and pully *asadero* cheese. Epazote can be found dried (it also makes a tea said to cure intestinal parasites), but it grows wild (even in Manhattan's Central Park, we're told), and with herb gardening on the rise, interested cooks may well choose to plant their own. We should also add that epazote in beans is reputed to reduce the flatulence caused by eating them. This is not, in our opinion, a reason to use, or not use, a delicious herb, but we wanted you to know just the same.

oregano

There is a great deal of confusion surrounding the use of the term Mexican oregano, although it appears that the one most commonly sold under that name is actually of the verbena family. When we think of Mexican oregano we think of an especially sharp, potent, and slightly resinous taste, and now that at least one national spice company is packing Mexican oregano for supermarkets, you can experience that taste. We prefer Mexican oregano for use in all the recipes in this book, although you can substitute ordinary oregano or a combination of oregano and marjoram if you wish. Be sure to finely crumble the dried herb between your fingers to release as much flavor as possible.

salsa

In 1991, sales of bottled salsa in the United States surpassed those of bottled catsup for the first time, a remarkably significant event. Based upon the easily concocted fresh table sauces of authentic Mexican cooking (see Chapter 1 for some typical recipes), these mixtures are simmered prior to canning, are usually tomato-based, and can range from fiery to mild, chunky to thin, excellent to awful. With its victory over catsup, salsa has become the mustard of the nineties, serving as a convenient, all-purpose flavor-boosting condiment with multiple uses. As salsa makers we couldn't be happier, and as cooks we've come to rely on the quick and easy bursts of flavor and color that bottled salsas add to even everyday food. One or more jars, of our brand or another, should be in the pantry of every cook interested in Southwestern food. If salsa is to be combined with several ingredients, select the hottest possible one you can find, in order that the fire remain evident in the finished dish.

tomatillos

These so-called Mexican green tomatoes are relatives of the ground cherry and the Cape gooseberry. The firm, round, green fruits, about the size of a large cherry tomato, are enclosed in crackly, paperlike husks which are removed before cooking. Commonly used raw or briefly cooked in salsas and sauces, the tomatillo has a tart, sour, berry flavor that does not take well to canning. Fortunately, fresh tomatillos keep well. Buy them, ideally firm and free of mold, and store them on a paper-towel-lined plate, unwrapped, in the refrigerator, where they will last for up to 3 weeks.

tomatoes

The tomatoes of Mexico are wonderful—medium-size, juicy, and sweet/tart, and they make everything prepared with them especially delicious. We supplement the supply that appears in our supermarkets by planting a goodly stand of tomatoes in our own garden, just in case. One can never have too many ripe tomatoes, whether cooking Southwestern or another cuisine. Away from the border, you are advised to seek out similar tomatoes (or to put in your own garden), and to spare no expense if you expect your salsas and other Southwestern fare to have authentic flavor and color.

Of course the turns of the seasons sometimes leave us relying on canned tomatoes, which are preferable to bland, mealy, and pale pink winter tomatoes in chili, soups, stews, and so on. We use plum tomatoes, preferably imported from Italy, and canned crushed tomatoes with added purée, depending on the recipe. Canned tomatoes should not be used in uncooked salsas—they are too sweet and soft.

tortillas

Even Diana Kennedy admits to being unable to make fresh corn tortillas by hand, needing a tortilla press to make things turn out right. We take that one step further and say that except for an afternoon spent experiencing the process firsthand in the kitchen of an excellent local cook, we don't make tortillas at all. El Paso (and to some extent the rest of the country) has reasonable—sometimes excellent—corn and flour tortillas in the supermarkets, and rather than cook no Southwestern food, we recommend you use them. Like the difference between good and great bread, the differences between tortillas are apparent but not usually fatal to the enjoyment of the meal.

Tortillas should be warmed, either to make them flexible and easier to handle or just to make them fresher-tasting and more palatable. There are terra-cotta tortilla warmers around, but we prefer to wrap tortillas in foil and heat them until steamy in a 300°F oven, 12 to 15 minutes. Put up several small packets if you will want tortillas throughout the meal and stagger the heating times. A microwave works well initially, but tortillas warmed in one turn almost immediately into stiff cardboard. Flour tortillas can also be warmed (and lightly toasted) on an ungreased griddle or over a charcoal or gas grill. Corn tortillas freeze well; flour tortillas do not. There are mail-order sources for all kinds of tortillas in the Appendix, and the quality of those will far exceed anything you find in a local supermarket.

mail-order sources for authentic ingredients

The El Paso Chile Company
909 Texas Avenue
El Paso, TX 79901
800-274-7468 or 915-544-3434

Prepared salsas, barbecue sauces, chili powder, Chile ristras, dried chiles, jalapeño jelly, condiments, snacks, gifts, Mexican chocolate, chipotles, moles, cajeta, basic ingredients, autographed cookbooks

Southwest Gourmet Gallery
320 North Highway 89A, #D
Sinagua Plaza
Sedona, AZ 86336
800-888-3484

El Paso Chile Company products, dried chiles, jalapeño jelly, blue cornmeal, red chile paste, chile ristras, chile seeds, gifts, basic ingredients

The Santa Cruz Chili and Spice Company
P.O. Box 177
Tumacacori, AZ 85640
602-398-2591

Red chile paste, unblended chili powders

Casados Farms
P.O. Box 1269
San Juan Pueblo, NM 87566
505-852-2433

Chimayo chili powder, chile ristras, blue cornmeal, basic ingredients

Josie's Best New Mexican Foods, Inc.
P.O. Box 5525
Santa Fe, NM 87502
505-983-6520

Blue corn tostaditas, blue cornmeal, chili powder, basic ingredients

Los Chileros de Nuevo Mexico
P.O. Box 6215
Santa Fe, NM 87502
505-471-6967

*Fresh and frozen green chiles, blue corn
tostaditas, blue cornmeal, dried chiles,
posole*

The Great Southwest Cuisine Catalog
1364 Rufina Circle, Suite 4
Santa Fe, NM 87501
800-869-9218

*El Paso Chile Company products, fresh and
frozen green chiles, posole, chile ristras,
dried chiles, Mexican chocolate,
chipotles, moles, cajeta, fresh corn and
flour tortillas, basic ingredients*

Bueno Foods
2001 Fourth Street SW
Albuquerque, NM 87102
505-243-2722

*Frozen hot and mild green chiles, red chile
paste, masa, posole, and basic
ingredients*

Texas Wild Game Co-operative
P.O. Box 530
Ingram, TX 78025
512-367-5875

Venison, other game meats

Night Bird Game and Poultry
650 San Mateo Avenue
San Bruno, CA 94066
415-543-6508

Game

Thundering Herd Buffalo Products
P.O. Box 1051
Reno, NV 89504
800-525-9730

Buffalo meat

D'Artagnan, Inc.
399–419 St. Paul Avenue
Jersey City, NJ 07306
800-327-8246 or 201-792-0748

Game

The Charcoal Companion
7955 Edgewater Drive
Oakland, CA 94621
510-632-2100

Wood smoking chips

New Mexico Brand
P.O. Box 159
Roswell, NM 88202
505-347-2572

Home-size green chile roasters

list of works consulted

"Bibliography" is too dry a word for the reading, cooking, and eating pleasure these books have provided. If you care about the cuisines of the Southwest and about the ingredients with which those cuisines are prepared, we urge you to enjoy these books.

Andrews, Jean. *Peppers.* Austin: University of Texas Press, 1984.

Bayless, Rick, with Deann Groen Bayless. *Authentic Mexican.* New York: William Morrow, 1987.

Creasy, Rosalind. *Cooking from the Garden.* San Francisco: Sierra Club Books, 1988.

Dent, Huntley. *The Feast of Santa Fe.* New York: Simon & Schuster, 1985.

Hutson, Lucinda. *The Herb Garden Cookbook.* Austin: Texas Monthly Press, 1987.

Jamison, Cheryl Alters, and Bill Jamison. *The Rancho de Chimayo Cookbook.* Boston: Harvard Common Press, 1991.

Junior League of El Paso, The. *Seasoned with Sun.* Rev. ed. El Paso: privately published, 1989.

Kennedy, Diana. *The Cuisines of Mexico.* Rev. ed. New York: Harper & Row, 1986.

———. *The Art of Mexican Cooking.* New York: Bantam, 1989.

———. *The Tortilla Book.* Rev. ed. New York: Harper Perennial, 1991.

McLaughlin, Michael. *The Manhattan Chili Co. Southwest American Cookbook.* New York: Crown, 1986.

Miller, Mark. *Coyote Cafe*. Berkeley: Ten Speed Press, 1989.

Peyton, James W. *El Norte*. Santa Fe: Red Crane Books, 1990.

Quintana, Patricia. *The Taste of Mexico*. New York: Stewart, Tabori and Chang, 1986.

Schneider, Elizabeth. *Uncommon Fruits and Vegetables*. New York: Harper & Row, 1986.

index